# AMERICA AT ITS BEST: OPPORTUNITIES IN THE NATIONAL GUARD

*by*

Col. Robert F. Collins, USA (Ret.)

THE ROSEN PUBLISHING GROUP, INC.
New York

Published in 1989 by The Rosen Publishing Group, Inc.
29 East 21st Street, New York, NY 10010

*First Edition*

Library of Congress Cataloging-In-Publication Data

Collins, Robert F., 1938–
    America at its best : opportunities in the National Guard / by
Robert F. Collins.
        p.    cm.
    Bibliography: p.
    Includes index.
    Summary: Discusses the history and role of the National Guard and
describes the requirements, obligations, and duties of service in
this organization.
    ISBN 0-8239-1024-5 : $14.95
    1. United States—National Guard—Vocational guidance—Juvenile
literature.   2. United States, Army—Reserves—Juvenile literature.
3. United States. Air Force—Reserves—Juvenile literature.
[1. United States—National Guard—Vocational guidance.
2. Vocational guidance.]   I. Title.
UA42.C673   1989
355.3′7′02373—dc20                                       89-32908
                                                              CIP
                                                               AC

This book is dedicated to the National Guard and the millions of young men and women who have served this country in the National Guard with honor, dedication, and courage.

# About the Author

Robert F. Collins is a recently retired officer who served more than twenty-five years in the US Army. He enlisted in the Army in 1960, graduated from Officer Candidate School in 1962, and achieved the rank of Colonel before his retirement in 1985. Col. Collins was in the Military Intelligence branch and served tours of duty in Korea, Vietnam, Germany, and the United States. He is a Soviet Foreign Area Officer with extensive travel in Eastern Europe and the Soviet Union. He taught US National Security Policy at the US Army's Command and General Staff College for five years and was a Professor of Military Science for two years. His decorations include the Army Commendation Medal, the Meritorious Service Medal, the Bronze Star, and the Legion of Merit.

# Acknowledgments

The author wishes to acknowledge the assistance provided by CPT Tom Schultz and SFC Tom Sherman. Both National Guardsmen provided needed materials and information about the Guard. Their cooperation and helpfulness is very much appreciated. Much of the material in this book has been drawn directly from military publications to insure both accuracy and currency. The author also acknowledges the information provided by the *National Guard Almanac*, an annual publication of Uniformed Services Almanac, Inc. Errors in the book, of course, are mine.

# Contents

# Introduction

Today's National Guard is a large modern organization that is essential to the nation's defense and one of the primary agencies that provide assistance to states during civil emergencies. The National Guard has a proud tradition of over 350 years of service to the country. It is a direct descendant of the militia and the Minutemen who served so well before and during the War of Independence. Indeed, today's National Guard is ready to turn out for service at a minute's notice.

The National Guard is a unique organization. It consists of two components: the Army National Guard (ARNG) and the Air National Guard (ANG).

The Army National Guard has been steadily expanding during recent years. The current assigned volunteer strength is over 450,000, with a projected goal for fiscal year 1992 of 465,500. The Guard represents approximately 32 percent of total Army strength and 43 percent of combat units. Today's Army Guard deploys in days, not months. Over 3,500 Army Guard units operate with a budget of over $5.2 billion. The inventory of buildings and facilities for the Army Guard has expanded to include 3,011 armories, 930 maintenance shops, 115 aviation support facilities, and 273 training sites.

The Air National Guard has an all-volunteer end strength of over 114,000. This represents approximately 14.3 percent of total Air Force strength and 26 percent of combat units. The Air Guard is deeply ingrained in the nation's economic and social life, having approximately 1,300 units in or near major cities in every state, the District of Columbia, Puerto Rico, the Virgin Islands, and Guam. With 24 wings (91 flying units) and 242 specialized mission support units, the Air National Guard today has its largest defense assignment in history. It is responsible for protecting, on an active day-to-day basis, most of the continental United States and Puerto Rico and has sole responsibility for the air defense of Hawaii. The Air National Guard, numerically the world's fifth largest air force, operates with a budget of more than $3.4 billion. The Air National Guard continues to receive new aircraft regularly with its authorization of over 1,560 planes. With 151 installations, including more than 5,000 buildings and other mission support structures, the Air National Guard's facility replacement value is greater than $9.1 billion.

The purpose of this book is to present in one volume information on the National Guard that will be helpful to young men and women who are considering enlisting in the Guard. It is hoped the book will be a useful guide to high school and college students, to their parents, to prior-service personnel, to high school guidance counselors, to active duty military education officers, and to the public at large.

It is possible to enlist in the National Guard before obtaining a high school diploma, but the Guard encourages all its members to obtain a high school education, and many career fields are closed to applicants without it. It is difficult to over-emphasize the importance of education as a vital ingredient in a successful National Guard career. You are well advised to obtain as much formal education as possible, up to and including graduate degrees. You should also take advantage of every opportunity to further your education by attending military or civilian courses offered through the Guard. The more education you have, the better your chances for promotion, whether as officer or enlisted member.

Enlisting in the National Guard does not mean a twenty- or thirty-year commitment. Indeed, the majority of enlistees serve a limited number of years and then return to their full-time civilian occupations. The great majority of former members state that they have profited greatly from their experiences in the Guard. Generally speaking, the Guard requires an initial eight-year commitment, with active participation ranging from three to eight years and the remainder of the period spent in inactive status. Of course, there are always exceptions, and that is why it is crucial that you understand all contractual obligations before signing any agreement with the National Guard. That does not imply that the Guard would attempt to have you sign something without your understanding it completely; in fact, the opposite is true. The Guard scrupulously avoids deceit or even the appearance of deceit in enlistment procedures.

One of the main points of this book is that you should obtain as much information as possible about the Guard before making the decision to enlist. You should talk to as many people as possible, including recruiters, teachers, parents, friends, former Guard members, and active Guard members. You should consider carefully all your obligations upon entering the Guard. You should also carefully examine your reasons for wanting to enlist. Enlisting on the spur of the moment or because there seems to be no other way out of personal problems is not a good way to get started in the Guard. Enlisting under pressure from friends or parents probably will not lead to either an enjoyable or a rewarding experience in the Guard. The decision must be yours, and yours alone.

Obtaining information about the National Guard is easy; the Guard is eager to provide information about the opportunities, benefits, obligations, and promotion chances associated with service. Recruiters can also furnish the latest information on training programs, bonuses, and opportunities. Talk to the Guard recruiter at length; it is a good idea to talk to him on several occasions. Prepare a list of questions about service in the Guard and have the recruiter answer them in detail.

No attempt is made to minimize the difficulties associated with adapting to military life, nor to soften the rigors of discipline required to complete basic training. The young men and women who can adapt to the demands of the Guard will be physically fit, morally sound, and socially adept. Most important, they will be strongly motivated to serve their country. Military service is demanding, and attrition rates are significant. The National Guard is an excellent place for many young people to grow and mature. It must be recognized, however, that the Guard is not for everyone. Some people, for whatever reasons, will never be comfortable nor find self-fulfillment in the Guard. The Guard also recognizes this fact and makes every effort to identify people not suited for service. It is in the best interests of both the individual and the Guard to separate those individuals quickly.

In the text the terms Guardsman and Guardsmen refer to both men and women. As you may have noticed, the military uses many abbreviations for the sake of brevity. The Appendix contains a list of those used by the National Guard.

# Chapter I

# General Military Information

The National Guard plays an important and unique role in the United States. The Guard has both a federal and a state mission. Functioning under the leadership of state governors, the Guard provides manpower, knowledge, experience, and equipment to assist in times of emergency, natural disaster, or civil turmoil. Guard personnel have assisted in fighting forest fires and floods and flown food, clothing, and medical supplies to regions isolated by floods, blizzards, hurricanes, tornadoes, and earthquakes. The Guard is there to assist in medical evacuation and search and rescue missions. The Guard provides support to drug and law enforcement agencies. The Guard gives help where help is required as part of its state mission. On the federal side of its mission, the Guard is a full partner in the nation's Total Force planning. Both Army National Guard and Air National Guard have worldwide missions and responsibilities as part of United States defense planning. Members of the Guard, called to active duty upon declaration of a national emergency, become members of the active duty military forces of the US and are assigned military missions.

Whether you intend to serve only a short time in the Guard or to make it a career, it is important to understand the place of the military in American society. The military plays a distinct role in the American form of government. It is a role that has been shaped by experience, tradition, and the unique American values of individual worth and personal freedom. The tradition of soldiery has not developed in the United States as it has in other countries. Indeed, from the very beginning of the American national experience it has been generally agreed that a large standing army was neither desired nor required. This belief was based on many circumstances. Starting with the colonial experience, the early American settlers, with hope for the future and tremendous optimism, were strongly independent and convinced that they were able to protect themselves. One of the reasons they had left Europe was to escape militarized, regimented, authoritarian societies; the American experience encouraged self-reliance, with security concerns best handled by oneself and one's neighbors. Consequently state militias, the direct forebears of the National Guard, were organized and functioning long before federal forces were formed. It is only since World War II that Americans have come to realize the necessity to have relatively large professional armed forces not only in place but also prepared to fight on short notice.

The United States has been blessed by its location. Until the beginning of the twentieth century it was relatively invulnerable to attack by foreign powers. Flanked by oceans on east and west and having friendly neighbors on the north and south, the United States developed its traditions and way of looking at the rest of the world in a secure, relatively isolated manner. An abundance of natural resources, a temperate climate, and productive agricultural lands further promoted its independence and self-reliance. The United States did not play a world role until this century, and no large standing military force was required to protect it from invaders, keep the sealanes open, or guarantee the freedom of the air. Conflicts were local and usually of short duration. When faced with an emergency, the American people rallied to the call for arms, fought bravely, and attempted to resolve the conflict quickly. The idea of the citizen soldier, which the National Guard embodies today, became an American legacy. Military leaders have emerged in time of crisis and received honor for their deeds, but the American people have always insisted that the citizen army be disbanded as soon as the crisis was over.

Americans have always been sensitive to the dangers of too strong a military influence on government. One of the bedrock tenets of our democracy, guaranteed by the Constitution, is civilian control of the military. It is an inviolable rule that the military only carries out policy; the military cannot make government policy. The role of the military is to advise civilian decision-makers and then to implement their decisions. A small professional force would be able to carry out most military missions, and troops could be mobilized for large-scale conflicts. This procedure worked well for the United States until this century, but now circumstances and the world situation have altered drastically.

The United States today is the acknowledged leader of the free world, with global responsibilities and obligations. The United States does not covet territory, nor is it militaristic; but it must have an adequate standing military force to protect its own interests and those of other democratic nations. Our boundaries, so secure for hundreds of years, are now vulnerable to attack from both the air and the sea. Our frontiers now extend to the Far East, to Africa, Europe, Asia, the Caribbean, and the Indian subcontinent. The world has grown much smaller thanks to technology and human progress. Events that occur in distant countries now have repercussions that directly affect the United States militarily, economically, and politically. It is no longer accurate to view the world as divided into communist and capitalist camps; other actors play important regional roles, and the balance of power is constantly shifting. Military personnel today not only must be technically and tactically proficient in their fighting skills, but they must also be aware of and sensitive to international relations.

The enlistee today and tomorrow faces unparalleled challenges: how to operate in an environment in which technology advances almost daily and military adversaries have the potential to destroy life as we know it. These challenges are all the more difficult because basically it is against the American character to prepare for a future war. We believe that conflicts should be resolved by discussion and reason, and force be used only as a last resort. We believe in the basic good of humanity and generally that our form of government and way of life are the best. We believe that government must serve the people and not vice versa. These are noble ideas, but we must remember that they are not shared by all governments around the world. Our world view works against programs to keep the military fully prepared on an immediate basis to respond to attack. The American tradition and ethic demand that the US can never be an aggressor, can never attack first, must conduct warfare in an honorable manner, and must be threatened significantly before resorting to violence. The US public must be kept informed of how the war is being conducted and must be able to see a prompt successful conclusion to the conflict.

These imperatives make service in the armed forces challenging and difficult. However, the main point about these conditions is that they are a genuine expression of the American character, and the military must operate within the bounds of public authority and approval. Because of these beliefs and the current world situation, maintaining reserve forces that are ready to go on a moment's notice is vital to the nation's security. During the last several years the missions and responsibilities assigned to the reserve forces have increased. The National Guard is playing an increasingly important role in defense planning.

Today's military members must be prepared to operate effectively anywhere along the spectrum of conflict. This could range from limited unconventional war or combatting terrorism to general nuclear war. The US policy in the nuclear age is one of deterrence. The armed forces must be strong enough to convince all potential aggressors that the benefits gained from aggression against the United States or its allies will not be worth the risks involved. Potential adversaries must also be convinced that the US will protect its interests. The likelihood of all-out nuclear war is very low in the foreseeable future; leaders of both the US and the Soviet Union realize that nuclear war has the potential to destroy life on earth. Recent agreements between the superpowers to dismantle certain classes of nuclear weapons underscore the seriousness of the problem. Still, the possibility exists of an unauthorized or accidental firing of a nuclear weapon or even a madman's choice to use a nuclear weapon. Having to cope with such a large range of possibilities imposes heavy burdens on the armed forces.

The highest probability of conflict in the near future in which selected units of the National Guard would be required to provide support would be low-level insurgencies and terrorist actions in areas far distant from the United States. An excellent example is the US commitment to protect US flag ships involved in oil operations in the Persian Gulf. Although a relatively low-level operation, it still poses dangers to the personnel involved. Many low-intensity conflicts have the potential to escalate into high-risk broader conflicts. Today's military must be prepared to operate effectively in Europe, Africa, Latin America, the Far East, and the Persian Gulf area. That is why the National Guard trains in locations and under different conditions all over the world.

During most of the history of this country, the military has been relatively isolated from the civilian community. Military personnel usually were stationed in isolated posts, served in foreign countries, or were stationed on ships at sea. There was no draft until this century, and not all sections of the public were fully represented in the military. As a result, the military knew very little about public concerns and perspectives, and the public in turn knew very little about military customs and traditions. The situation is quite different today, and the National Guard has played a part in having the military and the civilian community come to know each other better. The National Guard and other personnel in the Reserve forces are a "transmission belt" between the military and the civilian community. These citizen soldiers belong to both the military and the civilian community; they are able to bring new ideas and fresh perspectives into the military when called to active duty. Both sides benefit.

Close and continuing contacts exist between military people and civilians at innumerable levels. The media—newspapers, TV, radio, and movies—provide extensive coverage of military operations, research and development, budgets, training, educational requirements, and so on. In our democratic form of government, the people have a constitutional right to be informed of government activities—government in the sunshine. The Iran-Contra hearings revealed a great deal of wrongdoing, but the fact that seemed to draw the most ire from the American public was that so many things were done in secret without the knowledge of Congress and the public. Similarly, military undertakings, to be successful, must have the support of the people. Today's military member must understand that America's armed forces are truly a people's armed forces, and that he serves the American people as a whole and not any special-interest group. We learned many lessons from the Vietnam War, but the most important was that no war can be successfully prosecuted without the consent and active support of the US public.

The National Guard is truly representative of the society that it defends. It is a manifestation of the American ideal of the citizen soldier. Americans do not want a highly specialized, rigid, elitist group of mercenaries schooled only in military tactics to make up their armed forces. They do not want military automatons who react unquestioningly and unthinkingly to all orders. Rather, we want our armed forces to comprise well-educated young men and women who are idealistic, questioning, responsible, and representative of all sectors of society. We want our military to be strengthened by the constant infusion of bright young men and women who serve a limited time on active duty and then return to the civilian community with a better understanding of our nation's security needs. Both common sense and history tell us that the larger interests of a free society are best served by a military who are drawn from the society they serve, share its values, are broadly representative of the best that is in us, reflect the richness of our diverse origins, and are committed to the great and common purposes of our nation.

This then is a major contribution of the National Guard. The Guard guarantees that our military will be representative of the entire nation as well as bringing a productive vitality to our armed forces. We know that in time of need or in time of emergency, the Guard is there. It is indeed America at its best.

*Chapter* II

# History of the National Guard

The National Guard can trace its history back 353 years to December 13, 1636 (old-style calendar). On that date the General Court at Boston issued an order stating that all military men within the jurisdiction of the Court were to be ranked into three regiments. The oldest military units in the National Guard and the US Army are the Massachusetts units of the 181st Infantry, the 182nd Infantry, the 101st Field Artillery, and the 101st Engineer Battalion. In fact, these units are among the oldest military units in the world.

Virginia, Maryland, and Connecticut soon organized their units into regiments. The mission of the militia was to defend the settlement and colony in case of attack. Each militiaman was required to drill several times a month and to provide his own arms and equipment. As the threat of attack diminished, however, English colonial authorities began to use militiamen to augment regular troops in campaigns against French colonial possessions. During the French and Indian War several hundred militia officers gained valuable experience that they would use while serving in the Continental Army.

During the Revolutionary War, which began at Lexington and Concord on April 19, 1775, more than 164,000 militiamen from the thirteen colonies served under the command of the former Virginia colonel, George Washington. Without the militia, American independence could not have been won. While the Continental Army, with militia support, fought the main battles of the war, other militia regiments kept British forces in check by harassing, foraging, and raiding, limiting the royal troops to the cities. Thirty-one of today's Army National Guard units carry on their colors battle streamers embroidered with the names of the battles of the Revolutionary War.

After the war the militia was governed by the Militia Act of 1792. States were required to enroll men between the ages of eighteen and forty-five into companies, regiments, and brigades of militia. Each state was to appoint an adjutant general and brigade inspectors. As the enrolled or common militia declined in importance, the volunteer companies of the organized militia grew in strength. These units, which were uniformed, trained, and equipped, grew to a strength of 25,000 by 1804.

The name National Guard was first used in America by a New York militia unit on August 25, 1824. The name was a result of a visit to New York by the famous veteran of the Continental Army, the Marquis de Lafayette. The honor guard for the French hero, who had made great contributions to America's winning its independence, was made up of men from the 2nd Battalion, 11th Regiment of Artillery. This battalion had voted to rename itself the "Battalion of National Guards" in tribute to Lafayette's command of the Paris militia, *Garde Nationale*. The Battalion of National Guards later became the famous 7th Regiment, one of the nation's most distinguished militia organizations.

With the start of the War of 1812, the US Army consisted of only 10,000 men. The militia of the states was called into federal service, and more than 489,000 militiamen responded. Probably the most famous militia commander during the War of 1812 was Major General Andrew Jackson, whose backwoods sharpshooters defeated the British regulars in the Battle of New Orleans in 1815.

By 1850 the common militia, composed of all males between the ages of eighteen and forty-five, had been allowed to lapse. Most states recognized the volunteer militia companies—uniformed units that drilled on a regular basis—as the State Organized Militia. These units responded to President Lincoln's call in April 1861 for 75,000 militia to form the bulk of the Union Army for the first several months of the Civil War. No accurate figure can be determined as to the number of militiamen who fought in the Civil War. The figure of 1,933,779 is used for all volunteers who served in the Union Army. Many militia regiments that responded to the call of 1861 remained in service for the duration of the war. Other regiments returned to state status and served as cadres for the many volunteer regiments that the states furnished to the federal forces. Likewise, the initial bulk of the Confederate Army was made up of volunteer militia regiments. After the Civil War the National Guard was reorganized and grew to 90,000 men, largely commanded by officers who were Civil War veterans. Summer encampments became a regular feature, and the Regular Army began assigning advisers to each state.

With the outbreak of the Spanish-American War in 1898, close to 165,000 National Guardsmen volunteered for active duty. Only a few Guard regiments were sent to Cuba. One of the most famous was the Rough Riders who, under the command of Lt. Col. Theodore Roosevelt, assaulted San Juan Hill. Many Guardsmen were shipped to the Philippines to fight in the Philippine Insurrection.

The image of today's National Guard began to emerge in 1903, when congressional legislation (the Dick Act) required the government to play a more active role in organizing, training, and equipping the National Guard in line with the standards established for the regular Army. The Guard's involvement in aviation began in 1911, when New York's First Company, Signal Corps, became the first National Guard unit to get a plane off the ground. Soon thereafter

Guardsmen in Missouri and California established flying units. But it was not until 1915 that the National Guard's first federally recognized aviation unit, the 1st Aero Company of New York, came into being. A year later the new aviation unit was called to active duty along with the rest of the National Guard.

The Guard was again called into federal service in 1917 for World War I; more than 379,000 Guardsmen were ordered to active duty. During the war National Guard units throughout the country were organized into combat divisions of the American Expeditionary Forces (AEF) and soon afterward departed for France to enter combat. During the war the National Guard supplied seventeen combat divisions, or about 40 percent of the entire AEF. The accomplishments of the Guard units were highly lauded. National Guardsmen are credited with piercing the Hindenburg line, helping to crush the St. Mihiel salient, and smashing to victory through the Meuse-Argonne. The records of the German High Command, which were released after the war, noted that of the eight American divisions considered excellent or superior by the High Command, six were National Guard divisions. After the war, following a rapid and haphazard demobilization, it was necessary for many states to rebuild their National Guard units from scratch. The National Guard was reorganized to consist of four Cavalry divisions and eighteen Infantry divisions.

The National Defense Act of 1920 established the Army of the United States, to consist of the Regular Army, the Organized Reserve Corps, and the National Guard when called into federal service. Under this act, the Guard remained a state force and was commanded by state authorities. However, the act also provided for increased federal assistance for the Guard, meaning that when the units reached established Army standards of strength, equipment, and skill they were federally recognized and thus eligible for federal support.

The Congressional Act of June 15, 1933, created a new Army component, the National Guard of the United States. This component, while identical in personnel and organization with the National Guard of the several states, was a part of the Army at all times and as such could be ordered into active federal service by the President whenever Congress declared a national emergency. Thus it became possible for the National Guard to be given an Army mission without having to wait for a "call" to be issued through the various state governors.

In August 1940, President Roosevelt ordered the National Guard of the United States into active federal service. Between September 1940 and October 1941 the National Guard brought into federal service more than 300,000 men in eighteen combat divisions, as well as numerous nondivisional units including 4,800 men from the twenty-nine National Guard observation squadrons. The number of Guardsmen federalized doubled the strength of the active Army, and the National Guard observation squadrons, by their high state of training, helped to expand the US Army Air Forces. Not only did the Guard provide the Army with an experienced source of manpower, it also provided the expanding Army with leaders; over 75,000 National Guard enlisted men became commissioned officers during World War II, either through Officer Candidate School programs or by battlefield commissions.

During World War II, National Guard units participated in thirty-four separate campaigns and numerous assault landings in both the European and Pacific theaters of operation. Of the first five US Army divisions to enter offensive combat, four were National Guard divisions. One Guard division participated in the Normandy Omaha Beach D-Day landings on June 6, 1944. Guard units served well through-out the war; World War II casualties for National Guard divisions totaled over 185,000. With the end of the war in 1945, National Guard units were demobilized and personnel were returned directly to civilian life through Army separa-tion centers. Thus, for a short period during the winter of 1945–46 the National Guard ceased to exist.

The Secretary of War approved plans on October 13, 1945, calling for the reorganization of the National Guard. Under those "approved policies" the Guard was established with a dual mission and status. The National Guard of the United States (NGUS), as a reserve component of the Army of the United States (AUS), was to be an M-Day (Mobiliza-tion Day) force, thoroughly trained, equipped, and ready for immediate service in case of enemy aggression or a national emergency. The National Guard of the several states was to provide organizations and personnel for the Reserve (federal) Component and to preserve peace, order, and public safety in their respective states and during local emergencies. The approved policies also provided that the federal government was to supervise military instruction; furnish field training facilities, pay, uniforms, equipment, and ammunition; and contribute a fair portion of the ex-penses for the construction of National Guard armories. The federal assistance in armory construction marked an entirely new development in the history of the Guard.

The first four post-World War II Guard units were granted federal recognition on June 30, 1946. Also granted federal recognition on that date was the nation's first Air National Guard unit, the 120th Fighter Squadron of Colorado. In September 1947, with the establishment of the US Air Force, a new reserve component was established, the Air National Guard. Since that time the National Guard structure has consisted of both the Army and Air National Guard.

With the outbreak of the Korean War more than 183,000

Army and Air Guardsmen were called to active duty. Army Guard units included eight infantry divisions and three regimental combat teams. The Air Guard units called up include 22 wings and 66 tactical squadrons. During the war two Army Guard infantry divisions and four Air Guard wings were sent to Europe; four divisions and 17 wings remained in the United States; and two infantry divisions and two wings fought in Korea. Each of the Guard divisions was credited with four campaigns, and four of the 36 jet aces of the Korean War were Air Guard pilots.

In 1956 the various federal laws relating to the Armed Forces and the National Guard, including the National Defense Act of 1916, were codified in Title 10 and Title 32 of the United States Code (USC). As a result, all members of the Army National Guard and the Air National Guard are members of the Ready Reserve. Operating under Title 10, two Army Guard divisions and 104 other nondivisional units were mobilized during the Berlin Crisis of 1961–62; however, none were sent overseas. In the Air Guard call-up, 17 fighter squadrons, four recon squadrons, six air transport squadrons, one control group, and several supporting elements were activated. Within one month after mobilization, 216 Air National Guard jet fighters with supporting elements were deployed to Europe and assumed operational missions immediately upon arrival. All together, more than 67,000 members of the National Guard were mobilized.

During the Vietnam War, no massive call-ups of National Guard and Reserve units were made to raise military manpower. In January 1968, however, 11 Air National Guard units were ordered to active duty following the seizure of the *Pueblo* and the Lunar New Year (Tet) Communist attacks on South Vietnam. The call-up involved over 10,000 Air Guardsmen, including 560 pilots. In May 1968 two additional fighter units and one aeromedical unit, involving an additional 1,333 Air Guardsmen, were mobilized. Twenty units of the Army National Guard were ordered to active duty in May 1968. Of the more than 12,000 Army Guardsmen mobilized, more than 7,000 reported to Vietnam. All Air Guard units were demobilized in June 1969, and Army Guard units were demobilized in December 1969.

During the 1970s as America entered the all-volunteer era, the Army and Air National Guard began to receive more modern equipment and in larger quantities than it had in decades. The draft was abolished in 1973, and a major restructuring of active duty armed forces missions and Reserve missions was undertaken. Following the Army's "Steadfast" reorganization in 1972–73, nine Army Readiness Regions were set up throughout the United States, with Readiness Groups and subgroups established for each region. Under this program the Army greatly increased the manpower available to assist the Army Guard in advisory and training missions. The Army's "affiliation" program was initiated, whereby some Army Guard battalions and brigades were affiliated with active Army combat units with which they would mobilize and deploy. Newer helicopters and fixed-wing aircraft were received by the Army Guard in addition to upgraded tanks and artillery pieces, and infantry units replaced their recoilless rifles with TOW and Dragon anti-tank missiles.

During the 1970s the Air National Guard also underwent major changes in missions and aircraft. Phased out of its inventory were the C-124 Globemaster and C-121 Constellation cargo aircraft, the KC-97 aerial refuelers, and numerous F-100 fighter units. Replacing these aircraft were modern first-line C-130 Hercules cargo airlift, KC-135 jet tankers, and A-7D and A-10 tactical fighter units. Upon being assigned the KC-135 jet tankers, Air Guard aerial refueling units were assigned the mission of supporting year-round aerial refueling missions.

With more modern equipment and communications capabilities, the Guard was utilized more for state active duty missions in the 1970s than ever before. Floods, forest fires, tornadoes, snow emergencies, and energy shortages resulted in hundreds of call-ups. Civil disturbances, police and firemen's strikes, and walkouts by state prison employees resulted in other call-ups for domestic emergencies and to maintain safety and law and order.

As the Army and Air National Guard operate in the late 1980s and 1990s, they are better trained and equipped to respond to a state or national emergency than at any other time in their history. In recent years Guard units have received major new weapons and equipment. Their state of readiness and state of training are better than ever. The Guard is assuming more and more responsibility for the nation's defense. The Guard is growing and improving on a yearly basis. Today's Guard members are proudly carrying out the example and tradition of America's Minutemen.*

---

* This history of the National Guard has been adapted from the 1988 edition of the Army and Air *National Guard Almanac*, published by Uniformed Services Almanac, Inc., Washington, DC.

*Chapter* III

# General Information on the National Guard

No matter what line of work you are going into, it is always best to know as much as possible about your future employment. In this chapter you will find information about pay and benefits, commissioning opportunities, procedures for call to active duty, minority opportunities, promotions, retirement, and other programs. For more detailed information on all these programs and opportunities, talk to your recruiter.

As we have discussed, the National Guard has both a federal and a state mission. Simply stated, the federal mission is to train to be ready to augment America's active armed forces in the event of war or a national emergency; the state mission is to assist in protecting the lives and property of citizens in times of natural disaster, emergency, or civil disorder.

By law, National Guard units and individuals can be brought into active military service by several methods. The President can call National Guard units and members to active service whenever the United States, its territories, or possessions are invaded or in danger of invasion, when there is rebellion or danger of rebellion, or when necessary to carry out the laws of the United States. Under these circumstances, no congressional approval is required, and no warning or alert period need be given. During its period of service the National Guard retains its state character, even though it is a reserve component of the Army and Air Force. During such a situation, the state continues to appoint officers, and neither officers nor enlisted members may be held in service beyond the term of their existing commission or enlistment.

Another method by which National Guard members can be called to active duty is under provisions of Section 673 of Title 10 of the US Code. This law authorizes the President, after having declared a national emergency, to order any unit of the National Guard to active duty for not more than twenty-four consecutive months. In these circumstances members of the National Guard are ordered into federal service in their status as members of the Army or Air National Guard of the United States. The members of the federalized Guard units are relieved from duty in the National Guard so long as they remain in the active military service, and they are subject to laws and regulations applicable to members of the US Army and the US Air Force. They revert to the control of their respective states only upon release from active military service. Another law authorizes the President to order to active duty not more than 100,000 members of the Selected Reserve for a period not to exceed ninety days for purposes other than training. This action is authorized whether or not war or national emergency has been declared. The President is required to notify the Congress within twenty-four hours of his exercise of this authority and of the circumstances necessitating his action and the anticipated use of such forces. The law permits the activation of units of any size and of individuals not assigned to units. The call to active duty may be terminated by order of the President or by concurrent resolution of the Congress. Most of the time, when the Guard is called to active duty it is for state duty rather than federal duty.

*Pay and Benefits*

Numerous benefits accrue to members of the National Guard, both tangible and intangible. Intangible benefits resulting from serving in the Guard are substantial. Fortunately for the United States, many young men and women have high ideals and a deep sense of patriotism as well as a sincere desire to serve their fellow countrymen. These young people have a desire to contribute to the security of the United States and to render service to society. For most of them it is not a high-salaried job and material advantages that they are seeking, but an opportunity to serve a useful purpose in the world. Serving in the National Guard provides an opportunity to gain job satisfaction and to do something to serve America. The Guard will give you valuable leadership training and experience. As you progress in the Guard, you will be given more and more responsibility. You will learn specific skills of problem-solving, decision-making, planning, goal-setting, communicating, coordinating, supervising, evaluating, motivating, teaching, and counseling. You will learn the importance of teamwork and cooperation in getting a job done. You will learn to focus on the task at hand, and you will mature. You will learn to plan and utilize your time efficiently. These are all skills that transfer easily to the civilian sector. So whether you stay in the Guard for three years or thirty, you will benefit from the experience.

The accompanying table shows current pay scales for all the services. Military pay and benefits are set by Congress, which normally grants a cost-of-living increase each year. Enlistees can progress through nine enlisted pay grades during their career. Pay grade and length of service determine a member's pay.

The table shows the amount of pay for a single unit training assembly (UTA-1) and for multiple training assemblies (MUTA-4). After completion of basic and advanced individ-

# MONTHLY BASE PAY

| PAY GRADE | UNDER 2 | 2 | 3 | 4 | 6 | 8 | 10 | 12 | 14 | 16 | 18 | 20 | 22 | 26 |
|---|---|---|---|---|---|---|---|---|---|---|---|---|---|---|
| | | | | | YEARS OF SERVICE | | | | | | | | | |
| **COMMISSIONED OFFICERS** | | | | | | | | | | | | | | |
| 06 | | | | | | | | 3305.10 | 3417.30 | 3957.60 | 4159.80 | 4250.40 | 4496.70 | 4877.10 |
| 05 | | | | | | 2834.70 | 2920.50 | 3077.40 | 3283.80 | 3529.50 | 3732.00 | 3845.10 | 3979.20 | 3979.20 |
| 04 | | | | 2472.30 | 2518.20 | 2629.20 | 2808.60 | 2966.40 | 3102.00 | 3237.90 | 3327.60 | | | |
| 03 | 1768.80 | 1977.60 | 2114.10 | 2339.10 | 2451.00 | 2538.90 | 2676.30 | 2808.60 | 2877.90 | | | | | |
| 02 | 1542.30 | 1684.50 | 2023.50 | 2091.60 | 2135.40 | 2135.40 | | | | | | | | |
| 01 | 1338.90 | 1394.10 | 1684.50 | 1684.50 | | | | | | | | | | |
| **WARRANT OFFICERS** | | | | | | | | | | | | | | |
| W4 | 1802.10 | 1933.20 | 1933.20 | 1977.60 | 2067.30 | 2158.50 | 2249.10 | 2406.30 | 2518.20 | 2606.40 | 2676.30 | 2762.70 | 2855.10 | 3077.40 |
| W3 | 1637.70 | 1776.60 | 1776.60 | 1799.40 | 1820.40 | 1953.60 | 2067.30 | 2135.40 | 2202.90 | 2268.60 | 2339.10 | 2430.00 | 2518.20 | 2606.40 |
| W2 | 1434.30 | 1551.90 | 1551.90 | 1597.20 | 1684.50 | 1776.60 | 1844.10 | 1911.60 | 1977.60 | 2046.90 | 2114.10 | 2180.70 | 2268.60 | 2268.60 |
| W1 | 1195.20 | 1370.40 | 1370.40 | 1484.70 | 1551.90 | 1618.80 | 1684.50 | 1754.10 | 1820.40 | 1888.20 | 1953.60 | 2022.50 | | |
| **ENLISTED MEMBERS** | | | | | | | | | | | | | | |
| E9 | | | | | | | 2096.10 | 2143.50 | 2192.50 | 2242.20 | 2292.30 | 2337.00 | 2459.70 | 2698.80 |
| E8 | | | | | | 1758.00 | 1808.10 | 1855.80 | 1904.10 | 1954.20 | 1999.20 | 2048.40 | 2168.70 | 2410.20 |
| E7 | 1056.00 | 1324.80 | 1374.00 | 1422.00 | 1470.60 | 1517.40 | 1566.00 | 1614.60 | 1687.80 | 1735.80 | 1784.10 | 1807.20 | 1928.70 | 2168.70 |
| E6 | 926.70 | 1150.80 | 1198.80 | 1249.80 | 1296.30 | 1343.40 | 1392.90 | 1464.60 | 1510.50 | 1559.40 | 1583.10 | | | |
| E5 | 864.30 | 1008.60 | 1057.50 | 1103.70 | 1176.00 | 1224.00 | 1272.60 | 1319.40 | 1343.40 | | | | | |
| E4 | 814.20 | 912.60 | 966.30 | 1041.30 | 1082.40 | | | | | | | | | |
| E3 | 783.60 | 858.90 | 893.40 | 928.80 | | | | | | | | | | |
| E2 | 699.00 | | | | | | | | | | | | | |
| E1 | 646.20 | | | | | | | | | | | | | |
| E1u4 | | | | | | | | | | | | | | |

# WEEKEND PAY (MUTA 4)

| PAY SCALE | | | | | | | | | | | | | | |
|---|---|---|---|---|---|---|---|---|---|---|---|---|---|---|
| 06 | 235.84 | 263.68 | 281.88 | 311.88 | 335.76 | 350.56 | 389.40 | 410.32 | 455.64 | 527.68 | 554.64 | 566.72 | 599.56 | 650.28 |
| 05 | 205.64 | 224.60 | 269.80 | 278.88 | 326.80 | 338.52 | 374.48 | 395.52 | 437.84 | 470.60 | 497.60 | 512.68 | 530.56 | 530.56 |
| 04 | 178.52 | 185.88 | 224.60 | 224.60 | 284.72 | 284.72 | 356.84 | 374.48 | 413.60 | 431.72 | 443.68 | | | |
| 03 | | | | | | | | | 383.72 | | | | | |
| 02 | | | | | | | | | | | | | | |
| 01 | | | | | | | | | | | | | | |
| **WARRANT OFFICERS** | | | | | | | | | | | | | | |
| W4 | 240.28 | 257.76 | 257.76 | 263.68 | 275.64 | 287.80 | 299.88 | 320.84 | 335.76 | 347.52 | 356.84 | 368.36 | 380.68 | 410.32 |
| W3 | 218.36 | 236.88 | 236.88 | 239.92 | 242.72 | 260.48 | 275.64 | 284.72 | 293.72 | 302.48 | 311.88 | 324.00 | 335.76 | 347.52 |
| W2 | 191.24 | 206.92 | 206.92 | 212.96 | 224.60 | 236.88 | 245.88 | 254.88 | 263.68 | 272.92 | 281.88 | 290.76 | 302.48 | 302.48 |
| W1 | 159.36 | 182.72 | 182.72 | 197.96 | 206.92 | 215.84 | 224.60 | 233.88 | 242.72 | 251.76 | 260.48 | 269.80 | 269.80 | 269.80 |
| **ENLISTED MEMBERS** | | | | | | | | | | | | | | |
| E9 | | | | | | | 279.48 | 285.80 | 292.28 | 298.96 | 305.64 | 311.60 | 327.96 | 359.84 |
| E8 | | | | | | 234.40 | 241.08 | 247.44 | 253.88 | 260.56 | 266.56 | 273.12 | 289.16 | 321.36 |
| E7 | | 176.64 | 183.20 | 189.60 | 196.08 | 202.32 | 208.80 | 215.28 | 225.04 | 231.44 | 237.88 | 240.96 | 257.16 | 289.16 |
| E6 | 140.80 | 153.44 | 159.84 | 166.64 | 172.84 | 179.12 | 185.72 | 195.28 | 201.40 | 207.92 | 211.08 | | | |
| E5 | 123.56 | 134.48 | 141.00 | 147.16 | 156.80 | 163.20 | 169.68 | 175.92 | 179.12 | | | | | |
| E4 | 115.24 | 121.68 | 128.84 | 138.84 | 144.32 | | | | | | | | | |
| E3 | 108.56 | 114.52 | 119.12 | 123.84 | | | | | | | | | | |
| E2 | 104.48 | 104.48 | 104.48 | 104.48 | | | | | | | | | | |
| E1 | 93.20 | 93.20 | 93.20 | 93.20 | | | | | | | | | | |
| E1u4 | 86.18 | | | | | | | | | | | | | |

BAS for officers is $119.61 per month and $5.70 per day for enlisted personnel. When rations in kind are not available, the enlisted rate is $6.44 per day. When assigned to duty under emergency conditions where no messing facilities of the United States are available, the enlisted rate will be $8.53 per day. The rates for E1s under 4 months service are $5.27, $5.95 and $7.89 per day respectively.

## BAQ (Divide by 1/2 for A.T.)

### WITHOUT DEPENDENTS

| PAY GRADE | FULL | REBATE | WTH DEP. |
|---|---|---|---|
| 06 | 562.50 | 39.60 | 679.80 |
| 05 | 541.80 | 33.00 | 654.90 |
| 04 | 502.20 | 26.70 | 577.80 |
| 03 | 402.60 | 22.20 | 478.20 |
| 02 | 319.50 | 17.70 | 408.00 |
| 01 | 268.80 | 13.20 | 364.50 |
| W4 | 453.30 | 25.20 | 511.20 |
| W3 | 380.70 | 20.70 | 468.60 |
| W2 | 337.80 | 15.90 | 430.80 |
| W1 | 283.20 | 13.80 | 372.60 |
| E9 | 372.00 | 18.60 | 490.50 |
| E8 | 342.00 | 15.30 | 452.10 |
| E7 | 291.90 | 12.00 | 420.30 |
| E6 | 264.00 | 9.90 | 387.90 |
| E5 | 243.60 | 8.70 | 348.90 |
| E4 | 212.10 | 8.10 | 303.60 |
| E3 | 208.20 | 7.80 | 279.30 |
| E2 | 169.20 | 7.20 | 268.80 |
| E1 | 150.30 | 6.90 | 268.80 |

Insignia of the United States Armed Forces

| ENLISTED | | | | | | | | | |
|---|---|---|---|---|---|---|---|---|---|
| **PAY GRADE**<br>SERVICE | **E-1** | **E-2** | **E-3** | **E-4** | **E-5** | **E-6** | **E-7** | **E-8** | **E-9** |
| **A R M Y** | No Insignia<br>PRIVATE | PRIVATE | PRIVATE<br>FIRST CLASS | CORPORAL<br><br>SPECIALIST 4 | SERGEANT<br><br>SPECIALIST 5 | STAFF<br>SERGEANT<br><br>SPECIALIST 6 | SERGEANT<br>FIRST CLASS | FIRST<br>SERGEANT<br><br>MASTER<br>SERGEANT | COMMAND<br>SERGEANT<br>MAJOR<br><br>SERGEANT<br>MAJOR | SERGEANT<br>MAJOR<br>OF THE ARMY |
| **N A V Y** | SEAMAN<br>RECRUIT | SEAMAN<br>APPRENTICE | SEAMAN | PETTY OFFICER<br>THIRD CLASS | PETTY OFFICER<br>SECOND CLASS | PETTY OFFICER<br>FIRST CLASS | CHIEF<br>PETTY OFFICER | SENIOR CHIEF<br>PETTY OFFICER | MASTER CHIEF<br>PETTY OFFICER | MASTER CHIEF<br>PETTY OFFICER<br>OF THE NAVY |
| **A I R F O R C E** | No Insignia<br>AIRMAN BASIC | AIRMAN | AIRMAN<br>FIRST CLASS | SERGEANT<br><br>SENIOR<br>AIRMAN | STAFF<br>SERGEANT | TECHNICAL<br>SERGEANT | MASTER<br>SERGEANT | SENIOR<br>MASTER<br>SERGEANT | CHIEF<br>MASTER<br>SERGEANT | CHIEF MASTER<br>SERGEANT OF<br>THE AIR FORCE |
| **M A R I N E C O R P S** | No Insignia<br>PRIVATE | PRIVATE<br>FIRST CLASS | LANCE<br>CORPORAL | CORPORAL | SERGEANT | STAFF<br>SERGEANT | GUNNERY<br>SERGEANT | FIRST<br>SERGEANT<br><br>MASTER<br>SERGEANT | SERGEANT<br>MAJOR<br><br>MASTER<br>GUNNERY<br>SERGEANT | SERGEANT<br>MAJOR<br>OF THE<br>MARINE CORPS |
| **C O A S T G U A R D** | SEAMAN<br>RECRUIT | SEAMAN<br>APPRENTICE | SEAMAN | PETTY OFFICER<br>THIRD CLASS | PETTY OFFICER<br>SECOND CLASS | PETTY OFFICER<br>FIRST CLASS | CHIEF<br>PETTY OFFICER | SENIOR CHIEF<br>PETTY OFFICER | MASTER CHIEF<br>PETTY OFFICER | In addition all<br>enlisted personnel<br>shall wear the<br>Coast Guard<br>distinguishing<br>mark on the<br>right sleeve |

ual training, most Guard members will have 48 UTAs a year and 15 days of active training. Normally, each weekend drill consists of four unit training assemblies. A single UTA must be at least four hours in duration. Consequently, the Saturday and Sunday drills are full training days. Some National Guard units have provisions whereby members can spend Saturday night in the unit, but in most units members spend Saturday night at home and return on Sunday for the second drill day. Guard pay is subject to federal income tax, and most states require members of the National Guard and Reserve to pay state income tax on their Guard and Reserve pay. Daily pay rates for Guardsmen called to state active duty are determined by the state and may be less than, equal to, or greater than the Guardsmen's daily federal military pay rates. Information about state active duty pay rates and the various state tax exemptions for Guardsmen's pay can be obtained from your recruiter and local National Guard unit.

In addition to the pay received for weekend drills and 15-day annual training periods, some Guardsmen are eligible for special pay for aviation duty or hazardous duty. Hazardous duty includes such duties as aerial flights as noncrew member; parachute jumping; explosive demolitions duty; operation or duty as a crew member on submersible or research vehicles; experimental stress duty including working inside a high- or low-pressure chamber; and duty involving frequent and regular exposure to highly toxic pesticides or the servicing of aircraft or missiles with highly toxic fuels or propellants. Incentive pay of up to $100 a month can be awarded.

Special pay for proficiency may be paid to enlisted members designated as having special proficiency in military skills. There are currently two categories of proficiency pay: Shortage Specialty Pay and Special Duty Assignment Pay. Special Duty Assignment Pay is the major program and is authorized for personnel performing such voluntary duty as recruiter, drill instructor, pararescue, or career counselor, up to a maximum of $275 per month, depending on the proficiency rating of the person. Eligibility for these special types of pay depends on your qualifications and the duty position that you occupy in your Guard unit. There is also special incentive pay for officers in the National Guard who have specialized training or skills such as doctors, dentists, veterinarians, and optometrists. Be sure to talk to your recruiter if you have specialized skills.

Another benefit that attracts many people to the Guard is the retirement plan. Figuring the amount of retirement pay for Guardsmen is a very complicated process that factors in such items as attendance at weekend drills, active duty, completion of military correspondence courses, and attendance at military-related meetings and conferences. To be eligible to receive military retirement under the current system, you must: (1) complete twenty "satisfactory" years of federal military service, of which the last eight "satisfactory" years were served in the Guard; (2) reach age 60 before most retirement benefits can begin; and (3) not be entitled to receive military retired pay under other law. For a year to be "satisfactory" for retirement purposes, you have to earn a minimum of 50 points. Points are awarded for weekend drills, active duty, and other activities as mentioned above. The twenty "satisfactory" years need not be consecutive. Retirement pay is subject to federal income taxation. Retirement pay normally begins on the retiree's 60th birthday. If you meet all requirements, you would receive your retirement pay as long as you live. Tables that illustrate the amount of retirement pay based on grade and service are available at your recruiter's office.

As a member of the Guard you are eligible for federal benefits just as are members of the armed forces, but you are also eligible for state benefits. State benefits vary greatly: it is worth your time to look closely at those offered by your state. Enlistment/reenlistment bonuses, Guard scholarships and tuition assistance, state-funded Guard retirement pensions, improved medical benefits, legal assistance, and life insurance programs are among the benefits approved for Guardsmen by many states.

Guardsmen are eligible for federal benefits based on individual status. Benefits change depending on whether the Guard member is only attending drill, is on active duty, is in the Retired Guard under 60 years of age, or is in the Retired Guard over the age of 60. Among the benefits are use of post exchanges and commissaries (similar to department stores and grocery stores) that offer reduced prices; space-available travel on military aircraft in the US and overseas; use of military officer and noncommissioned officer clubs on military bases; and use of military clothing stores. Other benefits include legal assistance, use of military recreational facilities, use of military assistance facilities (USO) at major airports, low-cost life insurance, medical and dental support, certain Veterans Administration benefits, and eligibility for Survivor Benefit Plans. Regulations govern all these benefits plus others, but as a member of the Guard you can take advantage of them. In many cases your dependents are also eligible for some of the benefits.

*Promotions*

Both the Army and Air National Guard have promotion systems that reward members for outstanding performance of duty. Both organizations promote members who demonstrate the potential for more responsibility. Guardsmen who have no prior service can be promoted to the grade of E-2 after six months' service from the date of entry on initial active duty training. These personnel enter at the grade of E-1. Promotion to the grade of E-3 can be made without regard to unit vacancy. Normally, you need not appear before a promotion board for ranks E-2 through E-4. Once you have made E-4, you are administratively boarded for promotion. At the administrative promotion board the following factors are usually considered: military training, time-in-service, time-in-grade, civilian education, military education, military awards, and commander's evaluation. In both the Army and Air National Guard, unit vacancy is a critical factor for promotion, although under exceptional circumstances a member can be promoted to the next higher grade without a unit vacancy. For promotions to all grades, you must have a favorable recommendation from your unit commander, and you must have demonstrated proficiency in your Military Occupational Specialty (MOS) or Air Force Specialty Code (AFSC). As you progress in the Guard and receive promotions, you will fill increasingly more responsible positions within your unit. It is important to remember that promotions in the National Guard are not automatic; you must *earn* your stripes.

*Commissioning Programs*

Many rewards and benefits are to be gained by serving in the National Guard as an officer. You receive higher pay, gain additional responsibility, become more involved in the decision-making process within the unit, and develop your leadership skills. Both the Army and Air National Guard have programs open to enlisted personnel with no prior service that lead to a commission as an officer. Each service has its own requirements for its commissioning school as well as individual state requirements, but these are the basic requirements:

Age:   At least 18 years old at time of entrance into program, and not more than 30 years of age when accepting commission; maximum age can be raised in individual cases.

Mental:   Must achieve required levels on certain tests such as Armed Forces Qualification Test (AFQT), Officer Selection Battery (OSB), and Armed Services Vocational Aptitude Battery (ASVAB).

Character:   Be of high moral character (no run-ins with the law, no record of alcoholism, drug abuse, homosexuality, etc.).

Medical:   Pass an appointment type physical examination. Meet and maintain weight standards. Pass a physical fitness test.

Education:   Have a high school diploma or GED. Most programs now also require at least 60 hours of college credit to accept a commission.

Military training:   Must have completed both basic and advanced individual training.

While in Officer Candidate School (OCS) you will be paid in the grade of at least E-5.

Qualified applicants who have completed initial training and have been accepted into the OCS program may go to one of three different programs. They may attend the nine-week Reserve Component OCS, the 14-week active Army Branch Immaterial OCS, or the state OCS program. The state OCS program allows candidates to continue civilian employment while attending the course. Training is held one weekend a month for approximately one year.

The Air National Guard has a commissioning system that is national in character and centrally located at the Academy of Military Science at McGhee-Tyson Airport, Knoxville, Tennessee. Individuals selected for pilot training must complete a Basic Aptitudes Test (BAT) at Lackland Air Force Base (AFB), Texas. If the individual does not hold a private pilot license, the Flight Screening Program must be completed at Medina Annex to Lackland AFB. Then pilot and navigator applicants attend the Academy of Military

Science in Knoxville. Students attend the six-week course in pay grade E-5 or their current enlisted grade if higher. Upon graduation they are commissioned second lieutenants and go on to pilot or navigator training conducted at an Air Force base. Applicants for pilot/navigator training must enter flight training before age $27\frac{1}{2}$. Pilot training lasts about one year; navigator training, 33 weeks. After earning their wings, pilots and navigators take advanced courses in the aircraft used by their particular Air Guard unit. This instruction may last from 30 days to several months. Pilots incur a six-year commitment in the Air Guard after graduation, and navigators a five-year commitment.

Other applicants, in mission support rather than pilot/ navigator, also may attend the Academy of Military Science to obtain a commission. Upon graduation they are commissioned in the grade of second lieutenant, provided they have not reached the age of 35. When a college degree or completion of professional training is not required, the applicant must have at least two years of college and request a waiver for appointment.

The curriculum in both Army and Air programs is service-specific, but some common subjects are required of all officers. The courses help the applicants develop self-confidence and knowledge in their profession. There are many classes on leadership, world affairs, communication skills, supervision and management, and military skills. A great deal of the training is hands-on training.

The Army National Guard has several other commissioning programs. Helicopter flight training programs are available to commissioned and warrant officers and to warrant officer candidates. Applicants must meet stringent physical requirements and pass the Flight Aptitude Selection Test. Those applying for the warrant officer program receive appointments to the rank of warrant officer after completion of flight training. Warrant officer candidates attend a military development course for six weeks for beginning flight training. Helicopter flight training takes about nine months. Graduates incur a five-year obligation.

Special branches of the Army (Chaplain's Corps, Judge Advocate General's Corps, Medical, Dental, Veterinary, and Army Nurse Corps) account for all but a few direct appointments to the commissioned officer ranks. Highly technical skills in engineering, communications, or data management also qualify for direct appointment. Appointments in the special branches are made in the grade of first lieutenant through major based on military and civilian education and experience. Law limits direct appointments in all other branches to the grade of second lieutenant.

Warrant officer appointment requires warrant officer training prior to appointment and federal recognition. Each warrant officer candidate must complete Warrant Officer Candidate School (WOCS) and must be technically and tactically certified by the MOS proponent prior to appointment. The US Military Academy and the US Military Academy Prep School both have blocks of vacancies reserved for applicants from the Reserve forces. Applicants must meet all school prerequisites and then complete the four-year Military Academy course to obtain a commission. For more information about these schools, write to USMA, Director of Admissions, West Point, NY 10996; or to USMAPS, Chief of Admissions, Ft Monmouth, NJ 07703-5509.

Under a special program started in 1979, enlisted Guard members may enroll in advanced ROTC while still assigned to their Guard unit and receive both Guard pay and ROTC pay and allowances at the same time. For a college student who is a member of the National Guard and wants to become an officer, this Simultaneous Membership Program (SMP) is one of the best programs the military has to offer. To become a participant in the ARNG-ROTC SMP an individual must:

1. Be an enlisted member of the ARNG.
2. Be less than 30 years of age at the time of appointment.
3. Be enrolled in ROTC Advanced Course.
4. Have a minimum of four years remaining on enlistment obligation at time of enrollment into the SMP. Those with less than four years remaining on their National Guard enlistment may extend their enlistment to participate in the program.
5. Be enrolled or intend to enroll with a minimum of two years remaining in a full-time regular course of instruction leading to a baccalaureate or advanced degree at an eligible institution hosting or having a cross enlistment agreement with another institute hosting an Army ROTC program.

Young men and women joining the Army National Guard under the SMP are assigned to officer positions within a Guard unit, based on existing or projected commissioned officer shortages within the unit. The Guard officer trainees perform duties commensurate with the grade of second lieutenant, and they work under the close supervision of a commissioned officer. While enrolled in the SMP, Guard participants perform drills in the pay grade of E-5 or retain their current grade if higher. Once commissioned, they are paid as second lieutenants.

The Air National Guard also has a direct commissioning program. Direct commissions are open to men and women qualified to serve in chaplain, legal, and medical specialties. All applicants must have college or professional degrees except nurses, who must have graduated from a recognized school of nursing. Some age requirements are waived for direct commissions.

Air National Guard members may now enroll in Air Force ROTC programs as special students. It is not a mandatory program, but rather an agreement between the state Air National Guard and the Air Force ROTC unit. All pay, allowances, and uniforms are furnished by the Air Guard; instruction and materials are furnished by the affiliated ROTC program. Air Guard cadets remain Air Guard members throughout the training. They are paid with Air Guard funds and are eligible for state or Air Guard financial assistance. Once a baccalaureate degree is earned, the Air Guard member is commissioned in the Air National Guard of the United States. Air Guardsmen are eligible to apply for both Air Force ROTC and the Air Force Academy. Regulations govern each of these programs; your recruiter can explain them to you. For additional information, write to the AF ROTC unit at the college nearest you, or Registrar, US Air Force Academy, Colorado Springs, CO 80840.

### Organization of the National Guard Bureau

Organizational lines of command and responsibility run on separate tracks in National Guard units because of the dual federal and state missions. National Guard units are subordinate to state lines of command under normal conditions. Under declared states of emergency, Guard members become federalized and come under the control of the Army and Air Force.

The Chief, National Guard Bureau, reports to the Secretaries of the Army and Air Force through each of their chiefs of staff and is the Army's and Air Force's principal staff adviser on National Guard affairs. The National Guard Bureau formulates and administers programs to ensure the continued development and maintenance of Army and Air Guard units. As an operating agency, the National Guard Bureau is the channel of communication between the states and the Departments of the Army and Air Force.

The National Guard Bureau staff is directed by the Chief, NGB, and the director and deputy director of the Army and

Air National Guard, respectively. These positions are filled by National Guard general officers serving on statutory tours. The Chief, NGB, is nominated by the President and confirmed by the Senate. By law the authorized rank for this position is major general (two stars), but the past two chiefs have served as lieutenant generals (three stars). Also by law the position must be filled by a member of the National Guard. Both the Army and Air National Guard directors hold ranks of major general.

The National Guard Bureau consists of the office of the Chief; office of the Inspector General and a Joint Staff, comprising a director and seven joint offices serving both the ARNG and ANG staffs; the Army Guard Directorate, with seven specialized offices or divisions; and the Air Guard Directorate, with eleven specialized offices or divisions. The Army Guard Directorate and the Air Guard Directorate administer the personnel budget, facilities, training, and equipment for their respective services. The operating staff consists of Guard officers and enlisted members serving on statutory tours of active duty, Army and Air Force personnel, and Army and Air Force civilians. Total assigned strength of the operating staff is over 400, with more than half of the staff being made up of civilians. The Bureau performs an essential and difficult task by coordinating the efforts of the diverse state and territory National Guard organizations.

## Minority Membership

It is important to recognize the growing importance of the contributions women are making to national defense. Less than twenty years ago women made up only 2 percent of active duty personnel; today women make up about 10 percent. In the National Guard the same pattern has occurred. In recent years the number of minority group members has increased significantly. Membership in the Guard is open to eligible Americans of every race, color, and creed. The Guard has made tremendous efforts with gratifying results to increase its minority membership among women, blacks, Hispanics, Amerasians, American Indians, etc. The Guard has initiated several major recruiting programs to increase the attraction of Guard service to minorities. These programs target both enlisted and officer ranks. Opportunities for minorities have expanded greatly. Women are eligible to enter almost 90 percent of all military job specialties. Examples of the many occupations women are now entering include helicopter mechanic, air traffic controller, TV production specialist, heavy equipment operator, criminal investigator, and intelligence analyst. According to federal laws and policies, women may not be assigned to duty that involves a high exposure to direct combat: tank crew member, fighter pilot, infantryman, etc. However, despite these restrictions, the commitment to integrate women into the Guard has never been higher, and the outlook for all minorities in the Guard is bright. Currently, women comprise more than 6 percent of the Guard, and minorities comprise more than 20 percent, counting both enlisted and officer ranks. Discrimination, sexual harassment, and racial prejudice are not tolerated; in the National Guard you are judged solely on your ability and your performance.

### National Guard Technicians

The National Guard has developed a professional program to insure the smooth functioning of units at all times. Most of the activity at the units takes place during drill sessions and active duty training, but personnel are needed at all times to insure full-time continuity; National Guard technicians provide that continuity.

The concept of the program is that technicians form a full-time cadre that basically perform the same type of job in a technician status that they perform militarily. Thus, in case of mobilization they would carry their skills and training with them. Of the more than 50,000 technicians in the Guard, over 95 percent are referred to as military technicians because they must maintain military membership to hold their federal job. By regulation all military technicians must be militarily assigned to the same military unit by which employed, in a military specialty that is compatible with their full-time job, and maintain the military rank established for the full-time position.

Each State Adjutant General is the sole employing agent for technicians, with administrative controls and supervision retained at state level. The technicians work in a wide range of specialties and organizations. The majority perform technical work in supply, vehicle and aircraft maintenance, personnel, administration, accounting, contracting, examining, facilities management and maintenance, safety, unit readiness, training, program planning, program management, and program supervision. Although the Army Guard is four times larger than the Air Guard, the percentage of Air Guard technicians is greater because of the many ANG fighter interceptor, tactical fighter, and aerial refueling units that are manned around the clock and therefore have greater maintenance and flight crew requirements.

# Chapter IV

# Enlistment Qualifications and Procedures

The National Guard has established a system of enlisting that is extremely responsive to the differing situations of all its potential enlistees. As a result, you can plan your enlistment and attendance at basic training and advanced individual training to best suit your schedule. You can enlist and attend drills up to a year before going to basic training, you can enlist for a number of career specialties, you can split up your basic and advanced individual training, you can receive speeded-up promotions, and you can select your technical training. The important point is that you should have all your options explained by your recruiter. Besides the flexibility of starting basic training, cash bonuses are available for enlisting in certain career fields. You can receive credit for getting friends to enlist; you can receive credit for college hours completed. Some of these programs are described briefly in this book, but you owe it to yourself to have your recruiter explain in detail all the options available to you. Remember that you are a prized commodity; because all the services are voluntary today, competition is very keen to get young men and women to enlist. This is to your advantage because you are able to find the option in the Guard that is best for you. Enlistment options and procedures also may change as new programs are created or existing programs modified. Talk to your recruiter at length about what is available.

*Basic Qualifications for Enlistment*

Age

Non-prior service, 17 through 34 years of age. Parental or guardian consent required for persons under age 18. Prior service applicants must have sufficient service to allow them to complete 20 years of satisfactory service to include 8 years of qualifying service for retirement by age 60.

Education

All applicants must have a high school diploma or equivalency certificate. High school seniors who are within nine months of graduation may enlist and be paid for attending one Unit Training Assembly prior to graduation.

Citizenship

An applicant must be a citizen of the US or possess a valid Immigration and Naturalization Service Alien Registration Receipt Card, INS Form I-151.

Physical

All applicants must pass a complete medical examination and evaluation. Applicants must be of good moral character.

Aptitude

All applicants must pass the Armed Services Vocational Aptitude Battery (ASVAB). This test can be taken in high schools or at the Military Entrance Processing Stations (MEPS).

Service terms

The Army Guard offers enlistment options for men and women of 3, 4, 6, or 8 years active Guard and 2, 4, or 5 years in the Individual Ready Reserve (IRR) (nondrill status) or Inactive National Guard (ING). Options are available in accordance with current policy. The Air Guard offers two options: six years' active Guard or four years' active Guard and four years in the IRR (nondrill status). Enlistment options for prior service personnel vary slightly.

Active duty    Non-prior service personnel who enlist in either the Army or Air National Guard must complete a tour of active duty training (ADT) of at least 12 weeks. For males, the initial ADT requirement includes: (Army) attending basic training for eight weeks, followed by advanced individual training in the military occupational specialty for which they enlisted; (Air) attending basic military training for six weeks, followed by advanced training in the career field for which they enlisted. The number of weeks spent on instruction varies according to the specific course requirements for the career field. In all cases, however, 12 weeks is the minimum active duty training period. For Army Guard non-prior service females, the basic training period lasts for eight weeks, followed by the advanced individual training course for the career in which they enlisted.

The good moral character requirement establishes standards to screen out persons likely to become disciplinary problems. Standards cover court convictions, juvenile delinquency, arrests, drug use, homosexuality, deviant behavior, etc.

*Career Choices*

Besides being the largest employer in the nation, employing 1.8 million men and women, the military offers the widest choices of career opportunities. Together the five services, Army, Navy, Air Force, Marines, and Coast Guard, offer training and employment in over 2,000 enlisted job specialties. This means that for your enlistment in the Guard you have an extremely large number of career choices. These 2,000 specialties are divided into twelve broad occupational groups:

- Human services occupations
- Media and public affairs occupations
- Health care occupations
- Engineering, science, and technical occupations
- Administrative occupations
- Service occupations
- Vehicle and machinery mechanic occupations
- Electronic and electrical equipment repair occupations
- Construction occupations
- Machine operator and precision work occupations
- Transportation and material handling occupations
- Combat specialty occupations

Figure 1 shows the distribution of enlisted workers across the twelve occupational groups. This chart represents the distribution of occupations in all the services; however, the breakout is similar to the distribution of occupations in the Army and Air National Guard. Additional information about career fields and their civilian job equivalents can be found in the Appendix.

The population of a military base or a naval fleet often equals that of a small to mid-sized city. Like cities, the military needs many services, supplies, and utilities (such as

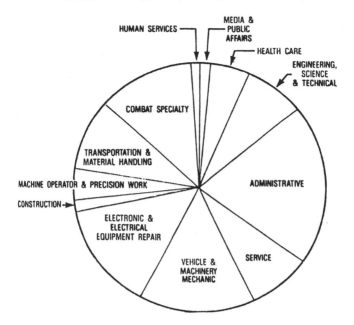

*Figure 1    Distribution of Enlisted Personnel by Occupational Cluster.*

electricity and communications) in order to be self-sufficient. Therefore, the services need a wide spectrum of occupations. Over three fourths of all military occupations have counterparts in the civilian world of work. For example, dental hygienist, air traffic controller, computer programmer, aircraft mechanic, and electronic technician occupations exist in both the military and civilian workforces. In fact, this great variety of jobs and job training provided by the military is the main reason most people give for enlisting in the armed forces and the National Guard. It is certainly true that the military offers some of the finest training available in the United States and has provided a good start for millions of young people. One other point of interest about Figure 1 is that it clearly shows how many support people are required to sustain the combat force. This percentage of combat personnel to support personnel is often called the "tooth to tail" ratio. It points up the fact that the great majority of personnel in the services and the National Guard are in support positions rather than combat positions.

Joining the National Guard involves entering into a legal agreement called an enlistment contract. The Guard agrees to provide a job, pay, benefits, and occupational training. In return, the enlistee agrees to serve for a certain period of time, which is called the service obligation. The standard National Guard service obligation is eight years for persons entering the Guard for the first time, regardless of age or sex. For the Army Guard the eight-year commitment can be completed in the following ways:

1. Eight years of membership in a unit, attending drills for six years and being paid for six years, with the remaining two years in the Individual Ready Reserve (IRR). (6 × 2 Program)
2. Four years of membership in a unit, attending drills for four years and being paid for four years, and four years in the Inactive National Guard (ING). (4 × 4 Program)
3. Three years of membership in a unit, attending drills for three years, and five years in the Inactive National Guard (ING). (3 × 5 Program)

For the Air Guard, non-prior service personnel can sign up for either six or four years active Guard, with the remainder of the eight years in the IRR (nondrill status). Active Guard means, with very few exceptions, attending a weekend drill (both Saturday and Sunday) once a month and 15 days of active duty with your unit each summer.

Enlistment programs vary for individuals. Major enlistment options include cash bonuses for enlisting in certain occupations, guaranteed choice of job training and assignments, and money guaranteed for college during and after service in the Guard. High school students often enlist during their senior year and enter basic training after graduation. The enlistment contract specifies the program selected by the applicant. It contains the enlistment date, term of enlistment, and other options such as a training program guarantee or a cash bonus. If, for whatever reason, the Guard cannot meet its part of the agreement (for example, to provide a specific type of training), the applicant is no longer bound by the contract. If the applicant accepts another enlistment program, a new contract is written. The National Guard always encourages young people to stay in high school and graduate. High school graduates are more likely to be successful in the Guard than nongraduates. Therefore, the Guard accepts very few nongraduates, and those few who are accepted are strongly encouraged to obtain their high school equivalency while in the Guard.

*Enlisting in the National Guard*

Entering the Guard can be treated as a four-step process:

Step 1: *Talking with a National Guard recruiter.* If you are interested in applying for the Guard, you must talk with a National Guard recruiter. Recruiters can provide detailed information about employment and training opportunities as well as answer questions about service life, enlistment options, and other topics. Recruiters are also able to provide the latest information on specific programs for the unit you will join. The programs and options available are not the same for all National Guard units. Different states offer different incentives for enlisting in the Guard. That is why it is so important to talk at length with your recruiter. If you decide to apply for entry and the recruiter identifies no problems (such as a severe health problem), the recruiter will examine your diploma or other educational credentials. You will then move on to the next step.

Step 2. *Qualifying for enlistment.* The procedure in determining your qualification for enlistment is basically straightforward. First, you complete a DD Form 1966, Application for Enlistment in the Armed Forces. This is only an application and does not commit you to enlist. The application requires information concerning your education, job history, residences, and other personal matters. Although it is voluntary, failure to complete all of the form may be grounds for not allowing you to enlist. From that point you will be required to take the ASVAB test either at your high school or at the MEPS nearest to you. You will also be required to have a complete physical examination to determine your physical qualification for enlistment. This will also be given at the MEPS. The mental and physical examinations are the key tools for determining the skills and areas that you are eligible to pursue as a member of the Guard.

Step 3. *Meeting with the Unit Administrator* (Service Classifier). After it is determined that you are physically, morally, and mentally qualified for enlistment in the Guard, the recruiter will take you to a unit where you will have an interview with the Unit Administrator. The Unit Administrator is a full-time employee who is responsible for running the unit in the absence of the Commander. Based upon that interview, you will determine three career fields in which you are qualified and interested in receiving training. You will then be taken back to the MEPS, where a Career Counselor will make the necessary reservations for the training desired and insure that your enlistment paperwork is completed expeditiously. Specifically, the classifier would enter your ASVAB scores into a computerized reservation service. Based on the scores, the system would show the career fields and training programs for which you qualify and when job training would be available. After discussing job training options with the counselor, you would select an occupation and schedule an enlistment date. Enlistment dates may be scheduled for up to one year in the future to coincide with job training openings.

Step 4. *Enlisting in the Guard.* After completing enlistment processing, you will be given the Oath of Enlistment into the Guard. The recruiter will then escort you to your unit (that day or at a time convenient for you), and you will be administratively processed into the unit. The Military Oath of Enlistment for both the Army and Air National Guard is as follows:

> I, _____, do solemnly swear (or affirm) that I will support and defend the Constitution of the United States and the State of _____ against all enemies, foreign and domestic; that I will bear true faith and allegiance to the same; and that I will obey the orders of the President of the United States and the Governor of _____ and the orders of the officers appointed over me, according to the laws and regulations. So help me God.

Once you have signed the oath, you are a member of the Guard.

There are certain incentive enlistment programs you should check out with your recruiter. Certain units in the Guard are authorized to pay enlistment incentives to non-prior service personnel. Additionally, certain career fields are authorized enlistment incentives regardless of the unit to which they are assigned. The enlistment incentive programs are as follows:

1. GI Bill—$5,040 GI Bill, which pays $140 per month for 36 months for a full-time college student.
2. Cash Enlistment Incentive—A person who selects this

incentive is authorized a $1,500 or $2,000 cash bonus.
3. National Guard Student Loan Repayment Program—
$10,000.

The National Guard also has programs that allow personnel to enlist in a higher grade than basic private E-1. Some
units have programs to reward people who are instrumental
in bringing friends into the unit. If you bring friends into
your unit, you could be promoted to Private E-2 or Private
First Class E-3.

If you have completed two years of a high school ROTC
program you can be promoted to Private E-2, and if you
have completed a three-year program you can enlist at grade
E-3, Private First Class. College students who enlist in the
Army Guard can join at pay grade E-2 or E-3. Non-prior
service college students with 20 to 29 semester hours may
enlist at E-2. Those with 30 to 59 semester hours or two
years of accredited college with no degree may enlist at E-3.
Non-prior service students with three or more years of a
four-year college program can join at E-3 and be promoted
to E-4 six months after entry into initial training. Students
with a degree can be promoted to E-4 four months after
entry into initial training.

Another unique program available in some Guard units is
the Civilian Acquired Skills Program. Under this program a
person who already possesses training or technical experience in a career for which the Guard has a counterpart may
be enlisted in the grade of Private First Class E-3. Career
fields covered include communications, medical, transportation, administration, calibration, construction, computers,
engineering, law enforcement, intelligence, and music.

One last piece of advice about enlisting is to visit a
National Guard unit before you make the final decision. The
Guard recruiter can make arrangements to take you to the

unit and return you home. He will introduce you to key persons who will assist you with any questions that you may have; this will help you obtain a better understanding of the National Guard program.

*Chapter* V

# Basic Training

You have completed all your enlistment and processing procedures. Now you are awaiting, usually with some anxiety, the start of your basic training—either Army or Air Force. The next two chapters will present information that will be useful to you in successfully completing these basic training programs. Remember that you are a member of the National Guard even while you are undergoing regular Army or Air Force training. You must complete basic training before you can begin your regular assigned duties with your National Guard unit.

Many erroneous ideas are held about basic training as well as about the military itself. Unfortunately, many ideas are based on what has been presented in post-Vietnam war movies, and not on reality. The image of brutal drill sergeants in basic training is more a creation of Hollywood than a depiction of real life. The vast majority of drill sergeants in the services are highly motivated, dedicated to their job and country, well trained, and interested in their trainees as individuals. The days of a military peopled by unthinking robots that blindly follow orders are long gone, if in fact they ever existed. Today the appeal of a military life as well as the appeal of the National Guard and Reserve units is on the rise. A renewed spirit of patriotism is evident among American citizens, after having reached a low point in the late 1960s and early 1970s during the Vietnam War. The end result is that the services and the National Guard seem to be attracting better educated, better qualified, and better motivated applicants than in the recent past. Because the National Guard can be more selective, it is all the more important that you know what is expected of you during basic training.

The military and the National Guard generally provide three kinds of training to personnel: recruit training, job training, and continuing education. Basic training differs in the Army and Air Force, but there are certain general similarities. Recruit training, usually called basic training, is a rigorous orientation to the military. Depending on the service, recruit training lasts from six to eleven weeks and provides a transition from civilian to military life. The services train recruits at selected military bases across the country. Where an enlistee trains depends on the service and the job training to be received. Through basic training recruits gain the pride, knowledge, discipline, and physical conditioning necessary to serve as members of the armed forces. Upon reporting for basic training, recruits are divided into training groups of forty to eighty people, meet their drill instructor, receive uniforms and equipment, and move into assigned quarters.

During basic training recruits receive instruction in health, first aid, and military skills. They also improve their fitness and stamina by participating in rigorous daily exercise and conditioning. To measure their conditioning progress, recruits are tested on sit-ups, push-ups, running, and body weight. All services require members to be physically fit and meet weight standards. In fact, some of the services do not allow enlistees to smoke in basic training as well as discouraging smoking by all members. Recruits follow a demanding schedule. Every day is carefully structured, with times for classes, meals, physical conditioning, and field instruction. Some free time (including time to attend religious services) is available. After completing basic training, recruits normally proceed to job training.

Basic training is physically, emotionally, and mentally demanding, but if you approach the training with the right attitude you can successfully complete it even if you have had no prior military experience. You must remind yourself that millions of young people have completed the training. You must focus on both short- and long-range goals. Your main goal is to complete the training; your short-term goal should be to do the best you can each day. The service wants you to succeed, and the military cadre will assist you in any way they can. In fact, if you feel that you need extra instruction in any phase of the training, the drill instructors will provide it.

The single most important thing in times of stress—and basic training is certainly a time of stress—is your attitude. In ninety-nine cases out of a hundred, if you think you can do something you will be able to do it. Tell yourself that no matter how tough the training is, you are going to see it through. As soon as you start feeling sorry for yourself or telling yourself that the training is too difficult, you are headed for trouble. Focus on the positive aspects of your training and how much you are learning. It is only natural that at times you will be discouraged, tired, and frustrated, but just recognize those feelings as passing phases and do not let them dominate your thinking. Focus on the personal rewards and satisfaction you will feel upon successful completion of the training. Your family and friends will be proud of you.

You will make some lasting friendships during basic training. The military wants you to develop a feeling of teamwork, pride, and camaraderie with the other members of your unit in your military career. You will find that basic training is a lot easier if you develop such friendships. If you can maintain your sense of humor and be enthusiastic about your situation, you are almost guaranteed to be successful. Basic training, like almost everything else in life, will be easier if you work with other people. Many NG units have a pre-basic training program that instructs non-prior service personnel on what to expect in basic. This is an excellent program to prepare you for basic. Check with your recruiter.

It is not my intention to minimize the rigors of basic training, but at the same time, do not enter into it with the idea that it will be too difficult for your abilities. You increase your chances dramatically for completing basic training by being in good physical condition. If you report in poor physical condition and overweight, the training will be very difficult. The military members who provide your training want you to succeed, just as do the members of your platoon, squadron, or company. You must tell yourself that military life is different from civilian life and be willing to learn, adapt, and change. Become interested in what is going on in your training; all services want their members to feel that they are part of the team. If you have questions about what is going on, ask the questions. If you feel that something is being done poorly or incorrectly, bring the subject up for discussion. That is not to say that all things will change or things will always go the way you think they should go, but you will have had input into those things that affect you personally.

Try to see basic training from the perspective of the particular military service. If, for example, we were to look at what the Army hopes to accomplish in basic training, we would see that it has a number of goals. The Army is interested in promptly identifying those men and women who would never be productive in the Army or would never be able to adapt to military life. The Army is also interested in providing realistic training that will be preparation for the hardships of combat. The Army must present training in military skills to a group of trainees the vast majority of whom have never had any exposure to the military. The Army must do this while instilling the values of esprit de corps, unit pride, and appreciation of Army traditions. And above all, the Army, like the other services, must be sensitive to the thoughts, feelings, and aspirations of the individual. The most important asset in all the services is the individual soldier, sailor, airman, or Guardsman. The services realize this. Training has to be conducted with the individual's welfare in mind.

If you understand what the military services are trying to do, you can appreciate that they have a difficult task. If you can understand their goals and then assist the service in accomplishing those goals, you will get through basic training with a great feeling of accomplishment and self-esteem. You will also have matured greatly. Now let's take a look at the basic training programs offered by the Army and the Air Force.

*Chapter* VI

# The US Army

*Mission*

The Army, along with the other services, has one fundamental mission: to provide for the security of the United States and for the support of US national and international policies. The ultimate purpose of all military training is to prepare personnel to carry out efficiently and expeditiously their service responsibilities. Title 10, United States Code, Section 3062, states in part:

> It is the intent of Congress to provide an Army that is capable, in conjunction with the other armed forces, of preserving the peace and security . . . of the United States; . . . supporting the national policies; . . . implementing the national objectives; . . . and overcoming any nations responsible for aggressive acts that imperil the peace and security of the United States.

The fundamental role of the Army, as the nation's land force, is to defeat enemy forces in land combat and to gain control of the land and its people. It is the traditional policy of the United States to maintain active armed forces of a size consistent with the immediate security needs of the nation. In the event of an emergency the armed forces must be capable of rapid expansion, and therefore military leaders and specialists must be trained during peacetime. This is the role the National Guard plays as part of its federal mission: to be always in a high state of training and readiness in the event the Guard must respond to an emergency in a foreign land. The mission of the Army is worldwide; therefore, the orientation of basic training has to incorporate this fact of world-wide responsibility into the instruction. The dynamic nature of international politics as well as the technology explosion with its concomitant improvements in weapons lethality make the Army mission more complex.

## Initial Processing

When all the enlistment procedures are completed and the day arrives for you to leave for basic training, it will be a day of excitement and anticipation. You will leave from the MEPS where you underwent your mental, medical, and administrative processing. If time has elapsed since your last visit to the MEPS, you will be interviewed as to any changes in your eligibility. Be sure to inform the interviewer of any medical or police involvement you may have had. You should always keep your National Guard recruiter informed of any change in your status or eligibility prior to going to basic training. You will then proceed to the Army Reception Battalion. As the name implies, this is where you are received into the training center. Normally, you can expect about a three-day stay at the Reception Battalion before picking up your new Army gear and being assigned to a training company.

Before starting basic training, you will go through Reception Battalion processing, which helps prepare new soldiers for training and later military life. Reception Battalion processing includes the following:

- Uniform issue and fitting
- Personnel records processing

- Identification (ID) card issue
- Orientation
- Eye and dental checks
- Casual pay
- Mental testing
- Interview
- Haircut (for men)

Orientation covers postal service, legal assistance, medical facilities, recreational facilities/activities, religious activities, leave and pass policies, post exchange facilities, medical care for dependents, financial care of dependents, movement of dependents, privately owned vehicles, visitors, correspondence, shipment of civilian clothing, pay and allowances, service obligations, allotments, survivors' benefits, and Servicemen's Group Life Insurance (SGLI).

Classes are given in barracks upkeep, physical training, drill (marching), and other subjects that will help you adjust to Army living. You will learn a great deal about the way the Army does things. Listen carefully and respond quickly and efficiently to instructions. After processing at the Reception Battalion, you proceed to basic training. Men and women receive essentially the same initial training, including weapons instruction, but may be trained separately. By regulation, women cannot be assigned to combat, but the Army believes that no matter what their specialty, soldiers should learn the basic combat skills that will give them the confidence and ability to defend themselves.

### Overview of Basic Training

The Army has developed a program for newly entering men and women that is both very general in scope for those who have no military experience and specific in nature when training soldiers for a designated Military Occupational

Specialty (MOS). All enlistees participate in Initial Entry Training (IET), which is designed to provide them with the skills and knowledge to perform the MOS in the first unit of assignment. Initial Entry Training includes Basic Combat Training (BCT), Advanced Individual Training (AIT), and One-Station Unit Training (OSUT). Basic Combat Training lasts eight weeks; Advanced Individual Training usually lasts nine weeks, although it may last longer depending on the individual skills being taught. One-Station Unit Training means that the initial entry training is conducted at one installation in one unit with the same cadre (instructors) and one program of instruction (POI). The BCT and AIT instruction are integrated to permit early introduction of MOS-specific training, followed by adequate reinforcement training to insure mastery.

The objective of IET is to develop a disciplined, motivated soldier who is qualified with a weapon, physically well conditioned, and drilled in the elements of soldiering. The objective of AIT is to provide the soldier with initial skills required to function effectively in the first unit of assignment. National Guard members are more likely to stay longer at their first unit of assignment than are members of the active duty Army. Men and women generally receive the same BCT and AIT.

Initial Entry Training is conducted in two ways. All combat and some combat-support soldiers attend One-Station Unit Training at one of the following locations:

- Infantry—Fort Benning, Georgia
- Armor—Fort Knox, Kentucky
- Field Artillery—Fort Sill, Oklahoma
- Air Defense Artillery—Fort Bliss, Texas
- Combat Engineer—Fort Leonard Wood, Missouri
- Military Police—Fort McClellan, Alabama

As mentioned above, the One-Unit Station Training provides both BCT and AIT. Soldiers in other occupational fields attend BCT for eight weeks, during which they learn common skills, then move on to AIT to learn occupational field skills. Basic Combat Training is given at Fort Dix, New Jersey; Fort Jackson, South Carolina; Fort Knox; Fort Leonard Wood; and Fort Sill.

Where you attend basic training depends on the terms of your National Guard enlistment agreement, the branch you chose to enter, and where you enlisted in the Guard. However, you will be told where you will take basic training; it will not be a surprise. Again, talk at length with your recruiter so that you are absolutely clear on the terms of your enlistment; this includes location of basic training, location of advanced training, and future assignment possibilities.

*Army Training Philosophy*

The Army states that you do not need to bring any special skills to basic training. If you have qualified for enlistment, the Army believes that the proper training will enable you to make the transition from civilian to military life. You are much better off if you are prepared for basic training by knowing what to expect and if you are in excellent physical condition when you report. Many unrealistic movies and articles about basic training portray the process as one in which the Army "tears you down and then builds you up again starting from scratch." In this version the Army degrades you and treats you with scorn until you prove how tough you are. The drill sergeants are mean and sadistic and are not accountable to anyone for their actions. As an individual trainee, you must be a "lone wolf," relying only on yourself and eventually proving your toughness by having a fight with the drill sergeant or another member of your platoon. Fortunately for today's military, this representation of basic training is completely false.

Military training, especially Basic Combat Training, respects the dignity and welfare of new soldiers. The Army objective is for the individual soldier to look back upon BCT with the feeling that valuable and rigorous training was conducted by competent professionals. The two cornerstones upon which the BCT program rests are that all soldiers must be capable of performing in a combat situation and that the new soldier must become a team-oriented individual. Team orientation must begin in BCT because it is so deeply a part of all Army operations, and yet it is not encountered in civilian society at large. In addition to these two cornerstones, the Army is concerned with several key issues as described in the BCT program of instruction.

First is the need for the program to be organized with formal intermediate goals or progressive phases so that the conversion process can be properly structured and both trainer and trainee can be clear on progress being achieved. Next is that training be conducted with as much realism, relevance, and combat fidelity as possible to better meet trainer expectations, but more important, to reduce the strangeness of the battlefield environment: sounds, weather, smells, sights, physical hardships, and excitement. The training must be carefully integrated and consistent so that the proper mix of knowledge, skill, and attitude elements are presented as they relate to each other.

It is the aim of training that every day in BCT be structured so that something new is presented, either initially or for evaluation. This takes the form of performance-oriented training requiring mastery of skills or new and different information. The challenge is to conduct the training so that the learning experience is success-oriented and confidence-building. The Army, like the other services, is extremely sensitive to the dignity of the new soldier. From the moment you take the Oath of Enlistment, whether as a member of the Guard or a member on active duty, you are a member of the armed forces, and you will be addressed as such. Every effort is made to instill in you a sense of identification with the uniform, with the training unit, and with the leaders of that unit. This is not accomplished in an atmosphere of "we/they." Rather, from the start of the training cycle you are in an atmosphere that emphasizes "leader/soldier," and the drill sergeant, committee group leaders, and officers want to be seen as role models to be emulated rather than persons to be feared or avoided.

Leaders of training units continually try to develop self-discipline in their soldiers. Development of self-discipline begins early in the BCT cycle through total control maintained by the training center cadre over all of your activities. The control is relaxed over time as you demonstrate that you are ready to accept responsibility for your actions. You are given ample opportunity to develop self-discipline.

Current Army doctrine organizes BCT into three distinct phases, each addressing a different segment of the soldierization process. These phases are:

I. Orientation and Soldierization (Trooper)
II. Weapons Training (Gunfighter)
III. Individual Tactical Training (Trailblazer)

Specifically, Phase I is characterized by the total cadre control of troops, absolute adherence to Army standards, constant supervision, platoon integrity, and the beginning of the soldierization process.

Phase II continues the enforcement of standards and heavily emphasizes Basic Rifle Marksmanship (BRM) and physical training. Additionally, Phase II features a transition from emphasis on platoon activities to emphasis on company activities. Generally speaking, a platoon has 30 to 40 trainees, and a training company has three or four platoons. A Phase II test completes this segment.

Phase III concentrates on Individual Tactical Training, field training, increased trainee leadership, increased self-discipline, continued company focus, and the end of Phase III test.

All previous training is then coordinated into a tactical field training exercise (FTX), an infiltration course exercise, and a 15-mile road march. Graduation and shipping to Advanced Individual Training complete the cycle. The training cadre evaluates and counsels each trainee regarding the goals and standards of each phase prior to his or her advancement to the next phase.

By using the phase concept and its inherent goals, the Army provides positive direction for young trainees through immediate short-term objectives. The drill sergeants and training cadre communicate the goals and standards for each phase. Goal-setting is fundamental to sound leadership, and constant feedback is vital to goal achievement. The phase training concept formalizes the soldierization process and defines shorter-term goals for all trainees. It establishes and clarifies goals for each phase and provides more structure to the leadership and counseling program. It also provides a workable format for a common-sense, cumulative approach to support the entire training process. The Army bases the soldierization process on an orderly and sequential method and hopes to produce disciplined, combat-skilled, and physically fit soldiers.

### General Information on Initial Entry Training

If you need one word to describe your first months in the military, the word would be *busy*. You will feel there are not enough hours in the day to accomplish what you have to do. Your entire duty day (Monday–Saturday) is highly structured and regimented. You get up about 5 a.m. and go to bed about 9:30 p.m., at least through the eight weeks of Basic Combat Training. You may feel that the Army is demanding too much of you, but remember that everybody else in your platoon probably feels the same way. You will learn to manage your time more effectively; you will learn the value of teamwork in accomplishing your assigned tasks. You will feel tired and rushed for the first several weeks. You will be dealing with information and situations almost totally unfamiliar to you. There will probably be times when you think you made the wrong decision in enlisting in the National Guard. You will want to blame everybody around you when things go wrong. The important thing to remember is that these or similar feelings are normal in stressful situations. Once you convince yourself that no matter how bad things get you are strong enough to overcome all obstacles, you have won the battle. You are on your way to becoming a soldier.

We spoke earlier of phasing in Basic Combat Training; the entire Initial Entry Training is also broken down into phases. Remember that BCT takes eight weeks, and the advanced individual training usually takes an additional nine weeks. On page 66 is a graphic representation of the five phases of IET. Abbreviations in the chart are as follows:

| | |
|---|---|
| D & C | Drill and Ceremonies |
| BRM | Basic Rifle Marksmanship |
| FTX | Field Training Exercise |
| MOS | Military Occupational Specialty |
| OSUT | One-Station Unit Training |

The buddy system (pairing of trainees for mutual assistance and support) is a part of IET. The system helps to reduce and cope with stress, teaches teamwork, and develops a sense of responsibility for fellow soldiers. You are formed

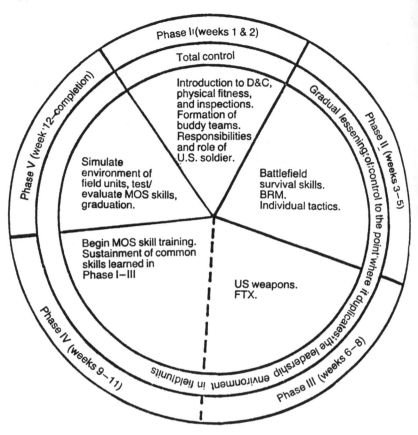

*Note:* IN OSUT, Phases III and IV may be combined.

*Figure 2*

into two- to three-person teams upon arrival at the training unit. You learn to help one another in all aspects of training. The system helps in the development of initiative, responsibility, and dependability. When possible, buddy teams participate together in training and other activities. Buddy team changes are limited during IET. Male-female buddy teams are not allowed.

Treatment of trainees follows very strict guidelines. Trainees are treated with the same fairness, respect, and dignity accorded to all soldiers. Degrading of trainees by use of vulgar, obscene, profane, humiliating, or racially or ethnically slanted language is expressly forbidden. Instructors and drill sergeants may touch trainees for the purpose of teaching proper performance. Physical contact for disciplinary or other reasons is prohibited. Sexual harassment is explicitly forbidden. In BCT training is conducted in all-male and all-female companies. In AIT male and female trainees are integrated at the group, class, or platoon level. Trainees are not allowed to wear civilian clothes at any time until they complete Phase III of IET. You are given the option of having the Army store your clothes or sending them home. Proper wearing of Army uniforms is taught in BCT. It is emphasized that it is a good idea to talk with someone who has recently completed BCT to get his or her impressions of the latest programs and procedures. Be sure to talk to your National Guard recruiter about the experiences of Guardsmen and women at BCT. It is better to have an idea of what is going to happen rather than being surprised by developments.

### Basic Combat Training Curriculum and Schedule

On the following pages the Basic Combat Training course is described in two ways: a course summary, and a weekly master schedule. Not all training programs are alike, but all follow the master schedule. Basic Combat Training is demanding, but if you are properly prepared you can complete it successfully and experience personal growth. Personal time is limited, but time is allowed to receive and answer mail, for personal care, and to attend church. You will successfully complete basic training if *you* want to.

You most assuredly will have the opportunity to travel

## BCT COURSE SUMMARY

| *Academic Time* | *Program Hours* |
|---|---|
| A. First Aid | 16 |
| B. Nuclear, Biological, and Chemical Defense | 8 |
| C. M16A1 Rifle Marksmanship | 62 |
| D. Hand Grenades | 8 |
| E. U.S. Weapons | 9 |
| F. Individual Tactical Training | 30 |
| G. Marches and Bivouacs | 16 |
| H. Physical Readiness Training | 50 |
| I. Guard Duty Training | 3 |
| J. Soldier Responsibilities and U.S. Army Heritage and Traditions | 2 |
| K. Identification, Preparation, and Wear of the Uniform | 2 |
| L. Inspections | 16 |
| M. Drill and Ceremonies/Platoon Drill Evaluation | 18 |
| N. Military Customs and Courtesies | 3 |
| O. Basic Military Communications | 4.5 |
| P. Military Justice | 1 |
| Q. Basic Map Reading | 8 |
| R. Code of Conduct | 1 |
| S. Threat Orientation | 1 |
| T. Law of Land Warfare | |
| U. Conditioning Obstacle Course | 4 |
| V. Confidence Obstacle Course | 3 |
| W. Rifle Bayonet Training | 10 |
| X. Hand-to-Hand Combat | 4 |
| Y. Personal Health and Hygiene | 1 |
| Z. Field Training Exercise | 19 |
| AA-1. Personal Affairs | 2 |
| AA-2. Alcohol and Drug Abuse Prevention and Control | .5 |
| AA-3. Equal Opportunity | 1 |
| AA-4. Personal Financial Management | .5 |
| Subtotal: | 303.5 |

| *Administrative Time* | |
|---|---|
| Company Commander Time | 4 |
| Reinforcement Time | 34 |
| CIF Issue | 2 |
| Uniform Fitting | 6 |
| Climate Orientation | .5 |
| Commander's Orientation | 1 |
| Immunization | 2 |
| Chaplain's Orientation | .5 |
| Equipment Turn-In | 3 |
| Payday Activities | 4 |
| Maintenance | 28 |
| Movement | 16.5 |

| | |
|---|---:|
| Inprocessing | 1 |
| Outprocessing | 1 |
| Graduation Activities | 4 |
| Guard Duty/Detail | 16 |
| National Holiday | 8 |
| Subtotal: | 131.5 |

*Examination Time*

| | |
|---|---:|
| Phase I Test | 2 |
| Phase II Test | 2 |
| Phase III Test | 5 |
| Subtotal: | 9 |

*Total Course Hours:*    445


## BCT RECOMMENDED MASTER SCHEDULE

| Week: | 1 | 2 | 3 | 4 | 5 | 6 | 7 | 8 | Total |
|---|---|---|---|---|---|---|---|---|---|
| First Aid | | 13 | 2 | | | | 1 | | 16 |
| Nuclear Biological Chemical | | | 8 | | | | | | 8 |
| Individual Tactical Training | | | 3 | | 10 | | 10 | 7 | 30 |
| Marches and Bivouacs | | 4 | | | | 4 | | 8 | 16 |
| Army Physical Readiness Test | 9 | 6.5 | 6 | 6 | 6.5 | 5 | 7 | 4 | 50 |
| Guard Duty | 3 | | | | | | | | 3 |
| Soldier Responsibility and US Army Heritage and Traditions | 2 | | | | | | | | 2 |
| Indentification, Preparation, and Wear of Uniform | 2 | | | | | | | | 2 |
| Inspections | 4 | 2 | 2 | 2 | 2 | 4 | | | 16 |
| Drill and Ceremonies | 7 | 4 | 3 | | 4 | | | | 18 |
| Military Customs and Courtesies | 3 | | | | | | | | 3 |
| Military Communications | 4.5 | | | | | | | | 4.5 |
| Military Justice | 1 | | | | | | | | 1 |
| Basic Map Reading | | | 4 | 4 | | | | | 8 |
| Code of Conduct | | | | | | 1 | | | 1 |
| Threat Orientation | | 1 | | | | | | | 1 |
| Law of Land Warfare | | | | | | 1 | | | 1 |
| Rifle Bayonet Training | | 3.5 | | | | | | | 3.5 |
| *Total* | 31 | 37.5 | 29 | 12 | 22.5 | 15 | 18 | 19 | 184 |

*An Army helicopter armament specialist readies an AH-64 Apache for flight.*

| | | | | | | | | | |
|---|---|---|---|---|---|---|---|---|---|
| Pugil Stick | | | 2 | 1.5 | | | | | 3.5 |
| Hand-to-Hand | | | 4 | | | | | | 4 |
| Conditioning Obstacle Course | 2 | | | | | 2 | | | 4 |
| Confidence Obstacle Course | | | 3 | | | | | | 3 |
| Personal Affairs | 2 | | | | | | | | 2 |
| Bayonet Assault Course | | | | | | 3 | | | 3 |
| Sure Pay | | | | | | | | .5 | .5 |
| Alcohol/Drug Abuse | .5 | | | | | | | | .5 |
| Equal Opportunity | 1 | | | | | | | | 1 |
| Personal Health and Hygiene | 1 | | | | | | | | 1 |
| Commander's Orientation | 1 | | | | | | | | 1 |
| Climate Orientation | .5 | | | | | | | | .5 |
| Chaplain's Orientation | .5 | | | | | | | | .5 |
| Field Training Exercise | | | | | | | 9 | 10 | 19 |
| Basic Rifle Marksmanship | 4 | | 4 | 34 | 12 | 6 | | 2 | 62 |
| Hand Grenades | | | | | 8 | | | | 8 |
| US Weapons Testing | | | | | | 9 | | | 9 |
| Phase I Test | | 2 | | | | | | | 2 |
| *Total* | 12.5 | 2 | 13 | 35.5 | 20 | 20 | 9 | 12.5 | 124.5 |
| | | | | | | | | | |
| Phase II Test | | | | | 2 | | | | 2 |
| Phase III Test | | | | | | | 5 | | 5 |
| Central Issue Facility | 2 | | | | | | | | 2 |
| Uniform Fitting | | | | | | 6 | | | 6 |
| Immunization | 2 | | | | | | | | 2 |
| Equipment Turn-In | | | | | | | | 3 | 3 |
| Payday Activities | | 2 | | | | | | 2 | 4 |
| Outprocessing | | | | | | | | 1 | 1 |
| Graduation Activities | | | | | | | | 4 | 4 |
| Company Time | | | | | | | 1 | 3 | 4 |
| Reinforcement Time | 3 | 9 | | | 8 | 5 | 9 | | 34 |
| Inprocessing | 1 | | | | | | | | 1 |
| Weapon/Equipment Maintenance | | | | | | | | 8 | 8 |
| *Total* | 8 | 11 | | | 10 | 11 | 15 | 21 | 76 |

while in the National Guard. You probably will have the opportunity to travel to places outside of the United States. You will meet many new people and form lasting friendships. You will be serving in an honored profession that offers promotions on merit and provides excellent job security. You will have almost unlimited educational opportunities and become part of an organization that cares for you and your family. I do not mean to imply that the National Guard is for everyone; that certainly is not the case. Some people cannot or will not adapt to military life. However, the vast majority of men and women who serve in the Guard say they are glad they served and feel stronger and more mature as a result of their experiences. For the young man or woman recently graduated from high school, the National Guard is a great place to start.

# Chapter VII

# The US Air Force

*Mission*

The mission of the Air Force is to provide an air arm that is capable, along with the other armed forces, of preserving the peace and security of the United States, providing for its defense, supporting national policies to carry out national objectives, and overcoming any nation responsible for aggressive acts that imperil the peace and security of the United States. In addition, the Air Force also provides major space research and development support for the Department of Defense and assists the National Aeronautics and Space Administration (NASA) in conducting the nation's space program. Teamed with the other armed forces, the Air Force is prepared to fight and win any war if deterrence fails.

The Air Force flies and maintains aircraft such as long-range bombers, supersonic fighters, Airborne Warning and Control Systems (AWACS) planes, and many others, whenever and wherever necessary to protect the interests of America and American allies. Over 575,000 disciplined, dedicated, and highly trained officers and airmen make up today's Air Force. Some of them pilot aircraft—everything from helicopters to the space shuttle. Many others do the jobs that support the Air Force's flying mission; they may work as firefighters, aircraft mechanics, security police, air traffic controllers, or in many other Air Force career fields. The Air Force currently recruits about 60,000 men and women each year to fill openings in hundreds of challenging careers.

*Overview of Initial Entry Procedures*

The Air Force provides two kinds of training to all enlistees: basic training and job training. All Basic Military Training is conducted at Lackland Air Force Base in San Antonio, Texas. BMT teaches enlistees to adjust to military life, both physically and mentally, and promotes pride in being a member of the Air Force. BMT lasts six weeks and consists of academic instruction, confidence courses, physical conditioning, and marksmanship training. After graduation from BMT, recruits receive job training in their chosen specialty.

Most BMT graduates go directly to one of the Air Training Command's Technical Centers for formal, in-residence training. In-residence job training is conducted at Chanute Air Force Base (AFB), Rantoul, Illinois; Keesler AFB, Biloxi, Mississippi; Lackland AFB, San Antonio; Lowry AFB, Denver, Colorado; Sheppard AFB, Wichita Falls, Texas; Goodfellow AFB, San Angelo, Texas; and several other locations nationwide. In formal classes and practice sessions, airmen learn the basic skills needed for first assignment in their specialty. Some Air Guardsmen may proceed directly back to their unit rather than going to the Technical Center; these personnel receive instruction in their skill through on-the-job training.

Air Force training does not end with your graduation from basic training or a technical training school. Upon return to your unit, you begin on-the-job training (OJT), a two-part program consisting of study and supervised job performance. Air Guardsmen enroll in skill-related correspondence courses to gain broad knowledge of their job, and they study technical orders and directives to learn specific tasks they must perform. They also work during weekend drills with their trainers and supervisors, who observe them during hands-on task performance. They are also offered advanced training and supplemental formal courses throughout their time in the Air National Guard to increase their skills in using specific equipment or techniques.

## What to Expect in Basic Training

In contrast to the Army, basic military training for the Air Force is conducted exclusively at one location. Lackland Air Force Base on the western outskirts of San Antonio is known as the Gateway to the Air Force. Basic training is a serious and highly important part of military life. From the day of your arrival through the rest of your military career, you will be expected to abide by training received in basic training as to conduct, actions, appearance, and all other aspects of military life. This training will give you the fundamental knowledge and skills required of a member of the Air Force and the Air National Guard. The subjects you will study include customs and courtesies of the Air Force, drill and ceremonies, military law, familiarization and use of weapons, the Air Force career system, the Military Code of Conduct, human relations, drug and alcohol abuse, and physical conditioning. All trainees, men and women, must fire an M-16 rifle as part of their training in the familiarization and use of weapons.

You will be expected to apply yourself diligently to all training and classroom activities. Your actions for the entire period of basic training and any subsequent technical training are carefully planned and programmed, and you will have very little free time. Normally you will be at Lackland AFB for about six weeks; however, your stay there could be extended for several reasons: illness, injury, recycle in training because of problems in academic areas or physical conditioning, poor attitude or adaptability rating, or changes in technical training requirements.

On your arrival at San Antonio International Airport, you are transported to the Air Force Military Training Center at Lackland AFB. There you are assigned to a training flight with about 45 other newly assigned airmen, taken to a dining hall for your first Air Force meal, and introduced to your military training instructor (MTI), who will escort you to your dormitory. This is where you will reside until completion of training. The following morning (unless you arrive on a weekend) is normally your first day of training. Other processing actions will follow during the remaining weeks of basic training. During basic training you are not allowed to use or park a privately owned vehicle (POV) on base. Following completion of basic training, you are provided transportation to your first base of assignment.

*Facilities*

Lackland has five chapels for the use of personnel. Worship services are held throughout the week for Protestant, Catholic, Jewish, and Orthodox faiths and several denominational groups. Other services include the American Red Cross, which is open twenty-four hours a day; Air Force Exchange service; three clubs with bingo, shows, dancing, television, radio, pool, Ping-Pong, reading room, and letter-writing facilities available; hobby shops; mail and postal service; banking facilities; Western Union; three theaters; and a library. Should you or your dependents require emergency financial assistance, you may seek help from the Air Force Aid Society through the personal affairs section of the consolidated base personnel office (CBPO).

*Physical Conditioning*

This very important part of basic training is accomplished through a program of supervised exercise and running.

Trainees who are unable to perform the required physical exercises and running are evaluated by a physical conditioning specialist and briefed on their specific weaknesses. Remedial exercises and running are prescribed as appropriate. If satisfactory progress is not made, trainees may be recycled in training until such time as they are able to perform the required evaluations. Running and marching are very much a part of basic training. You should condition yourself accordingly before enlistment to prevent possible foot and leg soreness. You should start a regular program of jogging before you go to basic. It is important that you participate in a program of exercise to stretch and strengthen your muscles such as swimming, tennis, basketball, or bicycling. Do not wait to start your conditioning program at basic; by then, it may be too late.

*Personal Matters*

*Homosexuality.* All the services are very strict about homosexuality; it is not tolerated in any degree in the Air Force. Participation in a homosexual act or proposing or attempting to do so is considered serious misbehavior. Similarly, airmen who have homosexual tendencies or who associate habitually with persons known to be homosexuals do not meet Air Force standards. No distinction is made between duty time and off-duty time; the moral standards of the service must be maintained at all times. It is the general policy to discharge members of the Air Force who fall within the purview of this policy. In certain circumstances trial by court-martial with possible punishment under the Uniform Code of Military Justice may be initiated. In recent years court cases have been brought against the services regarding regulations on homosexual behavior; in all cases so far the courts have ruled that the services can bar homosexuals.

*Pay and Clothing.* On the second training day men are

paid $130, and women are paid $230 (women are required to buy more items). This is advance partial pay, and some of it is used to buy items needed during the first few weeks of training (toilet articles, stamps, stationery, etc.). On the fifteenth day of training, you receive another $100. The remainder is paid to you on your thirtieth training day. You should take at least $25 with you for unforeseen expenses; enlistees arriving on Friday night or on a holiday are not paid until their second training day. You will receive a partial uniform issue during your first week and are then required to store all other outer civilian clothing. When you go for basic training take only enough clothing for a maximum of three days, but be sure it is adequate and suitable for the season. If you received an initial uniform issue from your Air National Guard unit within the last 90 days, you will receive only partial issue; therefore you should take your uniforms to basic training.

*Leave and Pass Policy.* Leaves during basic training and delay en route (leave between completion of basic training and beginning of technical training) are granted only for emergency reasons and must be verified by the American Red Cross. You should instruct your family to contact the Red Cross and provide full particulars of the emergency and your name, Social Security number, and military address. The Red Cross has trained personnel who can contact the proper officials at your Air Force base so that appropriate action can be taken. Calls to the National Guard Recruiting Office or to your unit commander will result only in unnecessary delay and expense. Neither routine leave nor delay en route will be granted because of normal pregnancy or childbirth, to get married, to resolve marital problems or threatened divorce, to resolve financial problems, because of psychoneurosis based on family separation, or to settle the estate of a deceased relative. Air Force rules cannot possibly cover all circumstances, so each request for leave during the initial training period is judged on an individual basis. You normally are authorized a one-day pass during your last week of training. These passes are for Saturday or Sunday from 9 a.m. (0900) to 8 p.m. (2000). Exceptions may be made in case of emergency. Off-base passes are considered a privilege and may be denied to all or part of a flight if not justified by acceptable training performance.

*Grooming Standards.* Members of the Air Force must maintain high standards of dress and personal appearance. The image of disciplined service men and women requires standardization and uniformity to exclude the extreme, the unusual, and the fad. Guidelines are required for the sake of neatness, cleanliness, safety, and military image. Therefore, uniforms must be kept clean, neat, correct in design and specifications, and in good condition. Shoes are required to be shined and in good repair. For men, hair and side-burns must be neat, clean, trimmed, and present a groomed appearance. Beards and goatees are not permitted except when specifically authorized for medical reasons. Mustaches are not permitted in basic training. While at basic training, women must keep their hair clean and styled to present an attractive appearance. The style must be such that the hair does not touch the lowest part of the collar or fall below the eyebrows. Accouterments such as pins and barrettes may be used only if plain, conservative, and similar in color to the person's hair. Earrings, including posts, are not worn with the uniform during basic training; however, posts may be worn at night.

*Excessive Weight.* If your weight exceeds the allowable maximum you will not be allowed to enlist at the MEPS. In fact, all the military services have weight standards that you must adhere to the entire time you are in the service. The weight standards are as follows:

### Weight Standards—Male and Female

| Height in | cm | Men Minimum | Maximum | Women Minimum | Maximum |
|---|---|---|---|---|---|
| 60 | 152.40 | 100 (45.45) | 153  (69.54) | 92 (41.48) | 130 (59.09) |
| 61 | 154.94 | 102 (46.36) | 155  (70.45) | 95 (43.18) | 132 (60.00) |
| 62 | 157.48 | 103 (46.81) | 158  (71.81) | 97 (44.09) | 134 (60.90) |
| 63 | 160.02 | 104 (47.27) | 160  (72.72) | 100 (45.45) | 136 (61.81) |
| 64 | 162.56 | 105 (47.72) | 164  (74.54) | 103 (46.81) | 139 (63.18) |
| 65 | 165.10 | 106 (48.18) | 169  (76.81) | 106 (48.18) | 144 (65.45) |
| 66 | 167.64 | 107 (48.63) | 174  (79.09) | 108 (49.09) | 148 (67.27) |
| 67 | 170.18 | 111 (50.45) | 179  (81.36) | 111 (50.45) | 152 (69.09) |
| 68 | 172.72 | 115 (52.27) | 184  (83.63) | 114 (51.81) | 156 (70.90) |
| 69 | 175.26 | 119 (54.09) | 189  (85.90) | 117 (53.18) | 161 (73.18) |
| 70 | 177.80 | 123 (55.90) | 194  (88.18) | 119 (54.09) | 165 (75.00) |
| 71 | 180.34 | 127 (57.72) | 199  (90.45) | 122 (55.45) | 169 (76.81) |
| 72 | 182.88 | 131 (59.54) | 205  (93.18) | 125 (56.81) | 174 (79.09) |
| 73 | 185.42 | 135 (61.36) | 211  (95.90) | 128 (58.18) | 179 (81.36) |
| 74 | 187.96 | 139 (63.18) | 218  (99.09) | 130 (59.09) | 185 (84.09) |
| 75 | 190.50 | 143 (65.00) | 224 (101.81) | 133 (60.45) | 190 (86.36) |
| 76 | 193.04 | 147 (66.81) | 230 (104.54) | 136 (61.81) | 196 (89.09) |
| 77 | 195.58 | 151 (68.63) | 236 (107.27) | 139 (63.18) | 201 (91.36) |
| 78 | 198.12 | 153 (69.54) | 242 (110.00) | 141 (64.09) | 206 (93.63) |
| 79 | 200.66 | 157 (71.36) | 248 (112.72) | 144 (65.45) | 211 (95.90) |
| 80 | 203.20 | 161 (73.18) | 254 (115.45) | 147 (66.81) | 216 (98.18) |

**(Weight in parentheses in kilograms)**

If your weight increases above the maximum allowable level while you are in basic training, you will be recycled in training until you meet the Air Force standards. Failure to meet Air Force standards could lead to discharge from the service.

*Medication.* If you are taking medication that was prescribed by a doctor, take it with the prescription to basic training. Female applicants who are taking birth control pills are encouraged to continue to take the medication. They should take their supply of pills to basic training even if the container does not bear a pharmacy label; they will be given refills or a new prescription.

*Mail.* Your specific military mailing address will be determined at Lackland. It is recommended that you do not request third-class mail (newspapers, magazines, etc.) to be forwarded to you during basic training, as your stay will be relatively short and another change of address will be needed when you depart. You should also discourage relatives and friends from sending packages that contain food, as food is prohibited in the dormitories.

*Chapel.* The chapel program is extensive and includes major faith groups and various denominational services each week. A chaplain will give you a thorough orientation briefing on all aspects of the religious programs on base and throughout the Air Force, plus a special focus on your personal adjustment to the Air Force life. You will also be given the opportunity to discuss with the chaplain any personal problems you may have. The Air Force has traditionally made a conscious effort to provide for the religious practices of all its members.

In this regard, each applicant should understand that special religious observance, diet, and other such practices may conflict with training schedules or essential operating procedures. If a conflict should arise, military training generally takes precedence. Major conflicts are resolved on an individual basis. Conflicts of this nature are rare after completion of the formal training phase at Lackland. Your National Guard unit usually is very accommodating in arranging working hours if you have other personal commitments.

### What to Take and What Not to Take

Take with you all prescription eyewear (prescription glasses or contact lenses). Contact lenses may not be worn

## Items Required during Basic Training

| Male | | Female | |
|---|---|---|---|
| *Mandatory Items* | | *Mandatory Items* | |
| * Flashlight w/reflective tape | | * Flashlight w/reflective tape | |
| ($2.15 aprx) | 1 each | ($2.15 aprx) | 1 each |
| * Padlock (pintumbler) ($4.30) | 1 each | * Padlock (pintumbler) ($4.30) | 1 each |
| Batteries ($.45 each) | 2 each | Batteries ($.45 each) | 2 each |
| Shoe polish (black) | 1 each | Shoe polish (black) | 1 each |
| Marking kit | 1 each | Marking kit | 1 each |
| Shoebrush | 1 each | Shoebrush | 1 each |
| Shine cloth | 1 each | Shine cloth | 1 each |
| Shower clogs | 1 pair | Shower clogs | 1 pair |
| Soap | 1 each | Soap | 1 each |
| ** Soap tray | 1 each | ** Soap tray | 1 each |
| Toothbrush | 1 each | Toothbrush | 1 each |
| Toothbrush tray | 1 each | Toothbrush tray | 1 each |
| Toothpaste or powder | 1 each | Toothpaste or powder | 1 each |
| Notebook | 1 each | Notebook | 1 each |
| Ballpoint pen | | Laundry soap | 1 box |
| (dark blue or black ink) | 1 each | *** Bras | 6 each |
| Laundry soap | 1 box | *** Underpants | 6 each |
| Zipper briefcase | 1 each | *** Shoes—pump, black | |
| Razor (may be electric) | 1 each | (calf or patent) | 1 pair |
| Blades (when safety | | Stockings (nylons/panty hose) | 6 pair |
| razor is used) | 1 package | Hairnet | 1 each |

82

Shaving cream
(when safety razor is used)
or shaving powder .......... 1 can
Laundry bag .......... 1 each
Deodorant .......... 1 each

*Recommended Items*

Shampoo .......... 1 each
Stationery .......... 1 each
Sewing kit .......... 1 each
Towels (if student doesn't have
sufficient number) .......... 2 each
Foot powder .......... 1 each
Cotton balls .......... 1 box
* Utility kit
(nail clippers and file) .......... 1 each
Aftershave lotion .......... 1 each
Iron .......... 1 each
Spray starch/fabric finish .......... 1 can
PC shirt (with squadron color
and number) .......... 1 each

* These items have been picked up and delivered by your instructor and will be paid for by you during your initial BX visit.
** Required if bar soap is used.
*** You will receive extra money during training for the purpose of purchasing these items either at BMTS or at your next duty station. We recommend you bring running shoes that are in good repair.

Zipper briefcase .......... 1 each
Ballpoint pen
(dark blue or black ink) .......... 1 each
Laundry bag .......... 1 each
Deodorant .......... 1 each
Sanitary napkins/tampons .......... 1 box
Shampoo .......... 1 each

*Recommended Items*

Stationery .......... 1 each
Sewing kit .......... 1 each
Towels .......... 2 each
Foot powder .......... 1 each
Cotton balls .......... 1 box
Lipstick or Chapstick .......... 1 each
Pressing cloth (man's handkerchief) .......... 1 each
Bathrobe .......... 1 each
Pajamas/nightgown .......... 1 each
Hairbrush .......... 1 each
Nail file .......... 1 each
Razor (may be electric) .......... 1 each
Eyeglasses guards .......... 1 each
Glass or cup .......... 1 each
Shoetrees .......... As required
PC shirt (with squadron color and number) .......... 1 each
Washcloth .......... 1 each
Iron .......... 1 each
Spray starch/fabric finish .......... 1 can

during basic training. You will be issued prescription glasses. The accompanying list shows the items enlistees are required to have during basic training. If you own suitable items you may take them with you.

You should take sufficient personal hygiene items to last for three days. It is recommended that you limit yourself to essentials, since you can purchase any items desired at reasonable prices after arrival. Your military training instructor (MTI) will determine whether items brought from home conform to the center's standards. Because space is limited, the items you take should be small or medium in size. The MTI normally arranges for pre-issue from the base exchange (BX) of a pintumbler type padlock and a flashlight. You will be required to pay for these items on your first visit to the BX.

Male enlistees are advised to dress casually and comfortably. Slacks, sport shirt, and jacket or sweater (depending on the season) are recommended. You should also wear comfortable shoes or sneakers. Take at least one change of underwear and socks and running shoes that are in good repair. Female enlistees are advised to dress modestly, casually, and comfortably. Wear a pantsuit or slacks or jeans with a blouse or sweater, a light raincoat, and comfortable, low-heeled walking shoes or tennis shoes (not platforms, high heels, or sandals). An extra change of clothing is necessary, as it could be four days before you are issued your Air Force uniform. You should also take a pair of running shoes in good shape.

You should not take expensive jewelry or sports equipment to the training center. Any medicine you have should be accompanied by a prescription from a medical doctor. Any weapons or dangerous instruments found in your possession or belongings will be confiscated and disposed of by Air Force personnel.

*Air Force Terminology*

You should know that all the services have their own individual expressions and abbreviations. It will not take long to learn the meanings; below are some of the words and phrases you will hear in basic:

| Air Force Term | Meaning |
| --- | --- |
| AI | Aptitude Index—an enlistment option with job classification during BMT. |
| Barracks | Dorm or dormitory where you live. |
| Blouse | Coat, usually the dress uniform. |
| BMT | Basic military training. |
| Boondocks | Woods or wilds, training area. |
| Bunk or rack | Bed. |
| BX | Base exchange, a store where you may buy everything from soap to shoes. |
| Colors | A national flag. |
| Cover | Hat. |
| Drill | To march, usually in a group. |
| Dining Hall/Chow Hall | Where you eat your meals. |
| Dorm/Dormitory | Building where you live. |
| Dispensary | A place for medical treatment (usually an annex to a hospital). |
| Esprit de corps | Spirit of camaraderie (in service to our country). |
| Flight | A unit of Air Force personnel; in BMT, approximately 47 persons. |
| GI | Government issue; members of all branches of the military are referred to as "GIs." |

| | |
|---|---|
| GTEP | Guaranteed Training Enlistment Program; an enlistment option that guarantees your job before enlistment. |
| Head | Bathroom. |
| Latrine | Bathroom. |
| Leave | Authorized vacation (30 days per year). |
| MTI | Military training instructor. |
| NCO | Noncommissioned officer. |
| NCOIC | NCO in Charge. |
| OIC | Officer in Charge. |
| Police up the area | Straighten up, make neat. |
| Quarters | A place to live, house, dorm, etc. |
| Rainbow | New basic trainee (because of multicolored attire of new arrivals). |
| Reveille | First assembly of the day, usually signaled by a bugle call. |
| Secure | Lock, close, put away. |
| Sick Call | A time to report to the dispensary for examination or treatment. |
| SP | Security policeman. This term is used for both security specialists and law enforcement specialists. |
| Squadron | An Air Force unit composed of at least two flights. |

*Daily Routine and Curriculum*

The thirty days of training, excluding Saturdays and Sundays, are extremely busy for the enlistees. You are not allowed liberty from your training area until the 15th day of training, and you are not allowed liberty off-base until after your 25th day. Basic training is a large-scale operation at Lackland. Approximately 200 to 400 men and women arrive daily to begin their military careers. During the first seven days the trainees are kept busy with job classification interviews, uniform fittings, testing, and other activities. You start your personnel records, which follow you throughout your career. You take tests, have medical and dental exams, and receive detailed orientation briefings. By the seventh day of training, classes begin. Your 12-hour days are full, consisting of academics, military training, and physical conditioning. Academic instruction includes Air Force organization and history, career advancement, financial management, customs and courtesies, human relations, group living, teamwork, illegal use of drugs, first aid, personal affairs and security, and various other subjects. In addition, all trainees go through the confidence course and fire the M-16 rifle.

The following is a broad outline of your daily schedule. It is a typical winter schedule; in the summer, physical conditioning is scheduled for the early morning.

| | |
|---|---|
| 0400–0500 | Military Training Instructors report for duty |
| 0500 | Duty day begins for trainees |
| Morning activities | Breakfast |
| | Processing |
| | Academic classes |
| | Military instruction |
| 1230 | Lunch |
| Afternoon activities | Parade |
| | Retreat |
| | Confidence Course |
| | Marksmanship |
| | Physical Conditioning |
| 1730 | Dinner |

# Male and Female Master Training Schedule

**1 DOT**
- 3 —Meals
- 1 —Dorm Arrangement
- 3 —Initial Clothing Issue
- 1.5 —Initial BX Visit
- 3 —24-Hour Orientation
- 1 —Buddy Briefing
- 1 —Pseudofolliculitis
- 1 —Military Training Time/Fire Drill
- .5 —Pay
- 1 —Clipper Cuts

**2 DOT**
- 3.5 —Meals/Reveille
- 3 —Medical Dental Proc.
- 1 —Immunizations/TB Time Test
- 2 —AFMET Testing/G.I. Bill
- 1 —Reporting Procedures
- 1 —Clothing Fit Insp.
- 2 —UCMJ Brg
- 1 —Dorm Arrangements
- 1 —Dorm Maintenance
- 1 —Individual Drill
- .5 —Personal Time

**3 DOT**
- 3.5 —Meals/Reveille
- 3 —Aptitude Testing
- 2 —Records Processing
- 2 —72-Hr Orientation
- 2 —Individual Drill

**6 DOT**
- 3.5 —Meals/Reveille
- 1 —1st Sgt Brg
- 4 —Interview Session
- 4 —ASVAB Testing
- 1 —Mail Call/MTI Brg
- 1 —Dorm Maintenance
- 1 —Study Time
- .5 —Personal Time

**7 DOT**
- 3.5 —Meals/Reveille
- 4 —Blood Donors
- 1 —Intro to Classroom Procedures
- 2 —Military Law
- 1 —G.I. Bill Brg
- 1 —Military Training Time
- 1 —Mail Call/MTI Brg
- 1 —Study Time
- 1 —Dorm Maintenance
- .5 —Personal Time

**8 DOT**
- 3.5 —Meals/Reveille
- 1 —Physical Fit/Rubella Immunizations
- 2 —Flight Drill
- 1 —Drug and Alcohol

**11 DOT**
- 3.5 —Meals/Reveille
- 1 —Physical Fitness
- 2 —Flight Drill
- 3 —Career Advancement
- 2 —Human Relations
- 1 —Mail Call/MTI Brg
- 1 —Study Time
- .5 —Personal Time
- 1 —Dorm Maintenance

**12 DOT**
- 3.5 —Meals/Reveille
- 1 —Physical Fitness
- 2 —Flight Drill
- 1 —Fitness Nutrition
- 4 —AF History & Org.
- 1 —Dorm Maintenance
- 1 —Military Training Time
- 1 —Mail Call/MTI Brg
- 1 —Study Time
- .5 —Personal Time

**13 DOT**
- 3.5 —Meals/Reveille
- 1 —Physical Fitness
- 2 —Flight Drill
- 2 —AF Security
- 1 —Open Ranks Insp

88

2 —Initial Marking
1 —Dorm Arrangements
1 —Dorm Arrangements
.5 —Patio Orientation

**4 DOT**
3.5 —Meals/Reveille
6 —Career Guidance (3 ANG, AFR Liaison Bfg)
2 —Physical Fitness Orientation (Prior to 5th DOT)
2 —Formal Dorm Guard Briefing (NLT 5TH)
1 —Immunizations/X-RAY
1.5 —Reading Test

**5 DOT**
3.5 —Meals/Reveille
1 —Physical Fitness
.5 —Blood Donors Bfg
1.5 —BMTS/CC Orientation
.5 —Chaplain Orientation
.5 —Dental Hygiene Bfg
1 —Sqdn/CC Briefing
2 —Sewing (Name/USAF)
1 —First Week Bfg
1 —Dorm Arrangement
.5 —Mail Call/MTI Bfg
2 —Patio Visit

2 —AF Customs/Courtesies
1 —Military Trng Time
2 —Military Trng Time
1.5 —Mail Call/MTI Bfg
1 —Dorm Arrangement
.5 —Personal Time
.5 —Grade Insignia

**9 DOT**
3.5 —Meals/Reveille
1 —Physical Fitness
8 —DD Form 398 Check
1 —Mail Call/MTI Bfg
1 —Study Time
.5 —Personal Time
1 —Dorm Maintenance

**10 DOT**
3.5 —Meals/Reveille
1 —Physical Fitness
2 —Flight Drill
4 —Assessments
1 —Standby Inspection
1 —Military Trng Time
1 —Mail Call/MTI Bfg
1 —Study Time
.5 —Personal Time
1 —Dorm Maintenance

(Wear of the Uniform)
2 —Moral Leadership
1 —Military Trng Time
1 —Military Trng Time
1 —Mail Call/MTI Bfg
1 —Study Time
.5 —Personal Time
1 —Dorm Maintenance

**14 DOT**
3.5 —Meals/Reveille
1 —Physical Fitness
3 —2nd Clothing Issue
1 —Final Marking
1 —Dorm Arrangement
2 —Military Trng Time
1 —Mail Call/MTI Bfg
1 —Study Time
1.5 —Personal Time
1 —Clothing Fit Insp

**15 DOT**
3.5 —Meals/Reveille
1 —Physical Fitness
2 —Flight Drill
1 —Pay/Allotment Proc
1 —ID Card Processing
1 —ID Base Lib Bfg
1 —Clipper Cuts (M)
   MTT (F)
1 —Peer Rating
1 —Weight Check
.5 —Military Trng Time
1 —Mail Call/MTI Bfg

1 —Individual Drill

SAT
3 —Meals
2 —Dorm Maintenance
8 —Military Trng Time
1 —Study Time
2 —Personal Time

SUN
3 —Meals
2 —Dorm Maintenance
2 —Religious Activities
4 —Military Trng Time
1 —Study Time
3 —Personal Time

SAT
3 —Meals
1 —Physical Fitness
5 —Military Trng Time
1 —Study Time
2 —Personal Time
2 —Individual Drill
2 —Dorm Maintenance

SUN
3 —Meals
2 —Religious Activities
5 —Military Trng time
1 —Study Time
2 —Personal Time
2 —Dorm Maintenance

SAT
3 —Meals
2 —Dorm Maintenance
8 —Military Trng Time
1 —Study Time
2 —Personal Time

SUN
3 —Meals
2 —Dorm Maintenance
2 —Religious Activities
5 —Military Trng Time
1 —Study Time
2 —Personal Time

SAT
3 —Meals
10 —Squadron Details
1 —Study Time
2 —Personal Time

SUN
3 —Meals
2 —Religious Activities
5 —Military Trng Time
1 —Study Time
2 —Personal Time
2 —Dorm Maintenance

1 —Study Time
1 —Personal Time

SAT
3 —Meals
2 —Dorm Maintenance
9 —Military Trng Time
2 —Personal Time

SUN
3 —Meals
2 —Dorm Maintenance
2 —Religious Activities
6 —Military Trng Time
2 —Personal Time

SAT
3 —Meals
8 —Student Details
2 —Military Trng Time
1 —Study Time

SUN
3 —Meals
2 —Religious Activities
4 —Military Trng Time
1 —Study Time
3 —Personal Time
2 —Dorm Maintenance

**16 DOT**
3 —Meals
12 —Student Details/KP
1 —Mail Call/MTI Bfg

**17 DOT**
3.5—Meals/Reveille
1 —Physical Fitness
2 —Flight Drill
3 —Rights/Freedoms/Resp
1 —Chemical Warfare
1 —Dorm Maintenance
2 —Military Trng Time
1 —Mail Call/MTI Brg
1 —Study Time
.5 —Personal Time

**18 DOT**
3.5—Meals/Reveille
1 —Physical Fitness
1 —Alterations P/U
1 —Clothing Fit Insp
2 —Hometown News Release

**21 DOT**
3.5—Meals/Reveille
1 —Physical Fitness
3 —Parade Practice
1 —Realterations Pick-Up
1 —Clothing Fit Insp
2 —AF Customs & Crts
1 —Dorm Maintenance
1 —Mail Call/MTI Brg
1 —Study Time
.5 —Personal Time
1 —Assignment Policies

**22 DOT**
3.5—Meals/Reveille
1 —Physical Fitness
2 —Sq Drill (Parade)
2 —Personal Affairs
1 —Open Ranks Insp (Wear of Uniform)
2 —Moral Leadership
1 —Dorm Maintenance
1 —Mail Call/MTI Brg
1 —Study Time
1.5 —Personal Time

**23 DOT**
3 —Meals
12 —Student Details/Dining Hall Attendants
1 —Mail Call/MTI Brg

**26 DOT**
3.5—Meals/Reveille
1 —Physical Fitness
1 —Clipper Cuts (M) MTT (F)
1 —Open Ranks Insp (Wear of Uniform)
1 —Sq Drill (Retreat Prac)
1 —Sq Drill (Retreat Cere)
3 —Military Trng Time
1 —Mail Call/MTI Brg
2.5 —Personal Time
* —MAS Brg
1 —Dorm Maintenance

**27 DOT**
3.5—Meals/Reveille
1 —Physical Fitness
2 —Written Evals
1 —Test Critique
1 —Dorm Arrangements
3 —Military Trng Time
1 —Mail Call/MTI Brg
1.5 —Personal Time
1 —Drill Evals
1 —Reporting Evals

**28 DOT**
3.5—Meals/Reveille
1 —Physical Fitness
2 —Orders P/U DDA Tech School Brg
2 —Military Trng Time
1 —Mail Call/MTI Brg

1 —Flt/Individual Pict
2 —Military Trng Time
1 —Mail Call/MTI Brg
.5—Resource Protection
.5—Confidence Crse Brg
1 —Study Time
.5—Personal Time
1 —Dorm Maintenance

19 DOT
3 —Meals
4 —Confidence Crse
5 —Premarksmanship Trng
.5—Military Trng Time
1 —Mail Call/MTI Brg
1 —Study Time
1.5—Personal Time

20 DOT
3.5—Meals/Reveille
5 —Marksmanship Trng
1 —Dorm Maintenance
1 —Mail Call/MTT Brg
1 —Study Time
1.5—Personal Time
1 —Standby Insp
2 —Self Aid/Buddy Care

24 DOT
3.5—Meals/Reveille
1 —Physical Fitness
2 —Sq Drill (Parade)
3 —Personal Affairs
1 —Dorm Maintenance
1 —Military Trng Time
1 —Mail Call/MTI Brg
1 —Study Time
2.5—Personal Time

25 DOT
3.5—Meals/Reveille
1 —Physical Fitness
3 —Parade
2 —Personal Affairs
1 —Town Pass Brg
1 —Dorm Maintenance
2 —Clothing Fit Insp (Last Look)
1 —Mail Call/MTI Brg
1 —Study Time
.5—Personal Time
* Traffic Safety Brg

2.5—Personal Time
3 —Parade
1 —Dorm Maintenance

29 DOT
3.5—Meals/Reveille
1 —Physical Fitness
1.5—Written Re Evals
2 —Departure Orien
1 —Sq Drill (Retreat Prac)
1 —Sq Drill (Retreat Cere)
1 —Dorm Maintenance
1 —Military Trng Time
1 —Mail Call/MTI Brg
2 —Personal Time
1 —Weight Check

30 DOT
3.5—Meals/Reveille
1 —Phys Fitness Re Evals
3 —Pay & Travel Arrg
1 —Immunizations
1 —Shipping Brg
2 —Dorm Dep Preparation
1 —Sq Clearance
1 —Mail Call/MTI Brg
2.5—Personal Time

Evening Activities    Military training/mail call
                      Study
                      Personal Time
2100                  Lights out

The training schedule will give you a good idea of the activities and classes you will be involved in at basic military training. There may be minor changes in each training cycle. (DOT = Day of Training).

Service in the Air National Guard means some of the finest technical training in the world. The Air Force, in the past and today, represents the leading edge of technology. The Air National Guard is an excellent place to gain valuable work experience. It is an exciting and rewarding place to start. By knowing what you are getting into and paying attention to what goes on at basic training, you will complete the program successfully.

# Conclusion

The appendix contains useful information regarding military occupations, a glossary of abbreviations, common questions and answers concerning your job rights, and other items concerning military customs and usage. Basic training is only your first step. Basic training is a difficult time, but it is relatively short. You must also look ahead and plan what you want to do in the rest of your career in the National Guard, whether it is just to serve your initial obligation or to make the Guard a thirty-year career. Many young people are not sure what they want to do with their lives when they graduate from high school. In fact, many people are not sure what they want to do with their lives when they graduate from college. Many feel that they need discipline and a sense of purpose, and the National Guard will provide that.

Probably the single most important attribute you can possess to have the best chance for a successful career in the National Guard is a positive attitude. Look on your time in the Guard as a learning experience and approach what you are going through with an open mind. Hard work and dedication to duty will always be rewarded. You will find that the National Guard can be professionally rewarding and personally satisfying.

Go into the National Guard with your eyes open. Find out as much as you can from the recruiter, former members, your counselor, and your parents before you make a commitment. Be sure you understand all the obligations incurred upon signing the enlistment papers. Look farther ahead than basic training. Plan on obtaining as much additional education as you can, both military and civilian, while you are in the Guard. Set your sights high. Look into the advantages of serving your country as as officer. You are embarking on a great adventure. Make the most of it.

# Appendix

## Army Occupations

Career fields are listed alphabetically, beginning with those combat-related groups closed to women (indicated by "C"). Those marked with an asterisk (*) are generally open to all applicants, but may include specific combat-related positions available only to men.

| Career Fields | Duties & Responsibilities | Qualifications | Examples of Civilian Jobs |
|---|---|---|---|
| Armor (C) | Performs combat tasks using tanks and armored reconnaissance vehicles. | Team sports, mechanical maintenance, orienteering. | Heavy equipment operator supervisor. |
| Combat Engineering (C) | Constructs and maintains roads and bridges; operates powered bridges; constructs minefields and installs booby traps, demolitions with high explosives; erects temporary shelters and sets up camouflage. | Automotive mechanics, carpentry, woodworking, mechanical drawing and drafting courses. | Blaster, construction equipment operator, construction supervisor, bridge repairer and lumber worker. |
| Infantry (C) | Performs combat tasks using rifles, mortars, tank destroying missiles, personnel carriers, vehicle-mounted guns and fire control equipment. | Team sports, orienteering, hunting and other outdoor sports. | Supervisor, gunsmith, security officer, firearms handler. |
| Administration | Performs general administrative duties such as typing, stenography and postal functions and specialized administrative duties | Basic clerical and communication abilities, typing, bookkeeping, stenography or office management skills desirable. | Clerk typist, secretary, employment interviewer, postal clerk, recreation specialist, office manager, personnel clerk, |

| | Description | Requirements | Related Civilian Jobs |
|---|---|---|---|
| | such as personnel, legal, club management, equal opportunity and chapel activities. | | bookkeeper, cashier, payroll clerk, court clerk, and restaurant or cafeteria manager. |
| **Aircraft Maintenance** | Performs the mechanical functions of maintenance, repair and modification of helicopters, turboprop, and reciprocating engine aircraft. | Considerable mechanical or electrical aptitude and manual dexterity. Shop mathematics and physics desirable. | Aircraft mechanic, plane inspector. |
| **Aircraft System Maintenance** | Performs maintenance of aircraft accessory systems, propulsion systems, armament systems, fabrication of metal materials used in aircraft structural repair and inspection and preservation. | Electrical and mechanical aptitude shop mathematics and shop work is desirable. | Aircraft mechanic, aircraft electrician, sheet metal machinist. |
| **Air Defense Artillery (\*)** | Emplaces, assembles, tests, maintains and fires air defense weapons systems; operates fire control equipment, radars, computers, automatic data transmission and associated power supply equipment. | Basic mechanical, electrical, electronic, mathematical abilities; emotional stability and high degree of reasoning ability. | Map and topographical drafter, cartographer. |
| **Air Defense Missile Maintenance** | Inspects, tests, maintains and repairs guided missile fire control equipment and related radar installations which guide missile to target. | Mathematics, physics, electricity and electronics. | Radio installation and repair inspector, electronic equipment technician, radio and TV repairer. |
| **Ammunition** | Handles, stores, reconditions and salvages ammunition, explosives, and components; locates, removes | Mechanical aptitude, attentiveness, good close vision, normal color discrimination. | Toxic chemical handler, ammunition inspector and acid plant operator. |

99

| Career Fields | Duties & Responsibilities | Qualifications | Examples of Civilian Jobs |
|---|---|---|---|
| | and destroys or salvages unexploded bombs and missiles. | manual dexterity and hand-eye coordination. | |
| Audiovisual | Operation of radio and television equipment, still and motion picture photography, audiovisual equipment repair and graphic illustration. | Install, inspect and maintain radio and television equipment, prepare illustrations, film and slide processing. | Cameraman, camera repair, photography, illustrator and studio accessories. |
| Automatic Data Processing | Operates a variety of electric accounting and automatic data processing equipment to produce personnel, supply, fiscal, medical, intelligence and other reports. | Reasoning and verbal ability, clerical aptitude, finger and manual dexterity and hand-eye coordination. Knowledge of typing and office machines. | Coding clerk, key punch, computer and sorting machine operator, machines records unit supervisor. |
| Aviation Communications-Electronic Systems Maintenance | Repairs and maintains navigation, flight control, and associated communications equipment. | Electrical/electronic theory and repair. | Electronics technician, radar repairer, electrical instrument mechanic repairer. |
| Aviation Operations | Maintains, installs and repairs aviation communication radar systems used for aircraft navigation and landing; performs air traffic control duties. | Mathematics and shop courses in electricity and electronics useful. | Radio and television or electrical instrument repairer, communication, electrical and electronics engineer and radio engineer. |
| Ballistic/Land Combat Missile and Light Air Defense Weapons System Maintenance | Inspects, tests, maintains and repairs tactical missile systems and related test equipment and trainers. | Mathematics, physics, electricity, electronics (radio and TV) and blueprint reading. | Electronic equipment technician, radio electrician and mechanic, TV repair and service technician. |
| Band | Plays brass, woodwind or percussion instrument in | Instrumental audition on brass, woodwind or percussion | Bandsperson, bandmaster, musician, accompanist, arranger, |

marching, concert, dance, stage and show bands, combos or instrumental ensembles. Sings in vocal group, writes and arranges music. — instrument. — music director, orchestrator, music teacher, orchestra leader and vocalist.

**Chemical** — Provides decontamination service after chemical, biological or radiological attacks, produces smoke for battlefield concealment, repairs chemical equipment and assists in overall planning of chemical, biological, or radiological activities. — Biology, chemistry and electricity. — Laboratory assistant (biological, chemical or radiological), pumper and repairer (chemical) and exterminator.

**Communications-Electronics Maintenance** — Installs, maintains radar and radio receiving, transmitting carrier and terminal equipment. — Electricity, mathematics, electronics and blueprint reading. — Radio control room technician, radio mechanic, transmitter, radio and TV repairer.

**Communications-Electronics Operations** — Installs, maintains field telephone switchboards and field radio communications equipment. — Mathematics, physics and shop courses in electricity. — Communications engineer assistant, plant electrician and radio electrician or operator.

**Electronic Warfare Cryptologic Operations** — Collects and analyzes electromagnetic emissions; performs electronic warfare duties in fixed or mobile operations. — Verbal and reasoning ability and perceptual speed; aural and visual acuity. — Radio and telegraph operator, navigator, intelligence research analyst, statistician, signal collection technician.

**Electronic Warfare Intercept Systems Maintenance** — Installs, operates and maintains intercept, electronic measuring and testing equipment. — Physics, mathematics, electricity, electronics (radio and TV) and blueprint reading. — Electrical instrument repairer and electronic equipment inspector.

**Finance and Accounting** — Maintains pay records of military personnel; prepares vouchers for payment; prepares reports, — Dexterity in the operation of business machines. Typing, mathematics, statistics and basic — Paymaster, cashier, statistical or audit clerk, accountant, budget clerk and bookkeeper.

| Career Fields | Duties & Responsibilities | Qualifications | Examples of Civilian Jobs |
|---|---|---|---|
| | disburses funds; accounts for funds, to include budgeting, allocation, auditing; compiles and analyzes statistical data and prepares cost analysis records. | principles of accounting desirable. High administrative aptitude mandatory. | |
| Field Artillery (*) | Operates, maintains and directs fire of field artillery guns, howitzers, missiles, rockets and related weapons. Operates and maintains supporting equipment such as target acquisition radars, sound and flash ranging, meteorological and survey equipment. | Emotional stability, mathematics and reasoning abilities. | Map and topographical drafter, cartographer, surveyor, weather chart preparer. |
| Food Service | Plans regular and special diet menus, cooks and bakes food in dining facilities and during field exercises. Serves as aide and cook on personal staff of general officer. | Home economics, work in a restaurant, bake shop or meat market. | Cook, chef, caterer, baker, butcher, kitchen supervisor and cafeteria manager. |
| General Engineering | Provides utilities and engineering services such as electric power production, building and roadway construction and maintenance, salvage activities, airstrip construction, firefighting and crash rescue operations. | Mechanical aptitude, emotional stability and ability to visualize spatial relationships. Carpentry, woodworking or mechanical drawing. | Carpenter, construction equipment operator, electrician, firefighter, driver, plumber, welder, bricklayer. |
| Mechanical Maintenance | Services and repairs land and amphibious wheel and track | Automotive mechanics, electricity, blueprint reading, | Automotive mechanic, motor analyst, bakery or refrigeration |

| | Description | Helpful school subjects | Related civilian jobs |
|---|---|---|---|
| | vehicles ranging from cars and light trucks to heavy tanks and self-propelled weapons; installs and repairs refrigeration, bakery and laundry equipment. | machine shop and physics. | equipment, repairer, frame, wheel alignment and tractor mechanic. |
| **Medical** | Assists or supports physicians, surgeons, nurses, dentists, psychologists, social workers, and veterinarians in 32 separate job classifications. Some provide direct patient care in hospitals and clinics, others make and repair eyeglasses, dentures, or orthomedical equipment, or maintain medical records. All play significant roles in a modern worldwide health care delivery system. | Biology, chemistry, hygiene, sociology, general math, algebra, animal care; knowledge of mechanics and electronics; general clinical skills. | Social worker (case aide), practical nurse, nurse's aide, dental assistant, surgeon's assistant, psychological aide, hospital attendant or orderly, veterinary assistant, food quality control, medical equipment repairer, medical or dental laboratory technician, physical therapy assistant, dietetic technician. |
| **Military Intelligence** | Gathers, translates, correlates and interprets information, including imagery, associated with military plans and operations. | English composition, typing, foreign languages, mathematics and geography. | Investigator, interpreter, records analyst, research workers and intelligence analyst (government). |
| **Military Police** | Enforces military regulations; protects facilities, roads and designated sensitive areas and personnel; controls traffic movement; guards military prisoners and enemy prisoners of war; investigates traffic accidents and crimes involving military personnel. | Sociology and demonstrated prowess and leadership in athletics and other group work helpful. | Police officer, plant guard, detective, investigator, crime detection laboratory assistant and ballistics expert. |

103

| Career Fields | Duties & Responsibilities | Qualifications | Examples of Civilian Jobs |
|---|---|---|---|
| Petroleum | Receives, stores, preserves and distributes bulk packaged petroleum products; performs standard physical and chemical tests of petroleum products; storage and distribution of purified water. | Hygiene, biology, physics, chemistry and mathematics. | Biological laboratory assistant, petroleum tester, chemical laboratory assistant. |
| Public Affairs | Prepares and disseminates news releases on military activities; prepares scripts, newsletters, announcements and public speaking engagements. | Clerical aptitude, verbal ability, clear speech and attentiveness. | Newspaper editor, editorial assistant, public information center. |
| Supply and Service | Receives, stores and issues individual, organizational and expendable supplies, equipment and spare parts; establishes, posts and maintains stock records; repairs and alters textile, canvas and leather supplies, rigs parachutes, decontaminates materials. Performs mortuary and grave registration functions. | Mathematical ability and perceptual speed in scanning and checking supply documents. Verbal ability; courses in bookkeeping, typing and office machine operations. | Inventory clerk, stock control clerk or supervisor, shipping or parts clerk, warehouse manager, parachute rigger and funeral attendant. |

| | | |
|---|---|---|
| **Topographic Engineering** | Performs land survey; produces construction drawings and plans, maps, charts, diagrams and illustrated material; constructs scale models of terrain and structures. Operates offset duplicators, presses and bindery equipment. Repairs survey instruments and reproduction equipment. | Mechanical drawing and drafting, blueprint reading, commercial art, fine arts, geography and mathematics. | Drafting (structural, mechanical and topographical), cartographic and art layout, model marker, commercial artist and physical geographer. |
| **Transportation** | Operates and performs preventive maintenance on passenger, light, medium and heavy cargo vehicles; operates and maintains marine harbor craft; performs as air traffic controller. | Mechanical aptitude, manual dexterity, eye/hand coordination, FAA certification for air traffic control, license for vehicle operation. | Truck driver, FAA air traffic controller. |

## Air Force Occupations

| Career Fields | Duties & Responsibilities | Qualifications | Examples of Civilian Jobs |
|---|---|---|---|
| **Accounting, Finance and Auditing** | Prepares documents required to account for and disburse funds, including budgeting allocation, disbursing, auditing and preparing cost analysis records. | Dexterity in the operation of business machines. Typing, mathematics, statistics and accounting desirable. High administrative aptitude mandatory. | Public accountant, auditor, bookkeeper, budget clerk and paymaster. |
| **Administration** | Prepares correspondence, statistical summaries, arranges priority and distribution systems, maintains files, prepares and consolidates reports and arranges for graphic presentation. | Business, English, typing and mathematics courses desirable. | Clerk typist, file secretary, stenographer, receptionist. |
| **Aircraft Maintenance** | Performs the mechanical functions of maintenance, repair, and modification of helicopters, turboprop, reciprocating engine and jet aircraft. | Considerable mechanical or electrical aptitude and manual dexterity. Physics, hydraulics, electronics, mechanics and mathematics desirable. | Aircraft mechanic, airframe inspector. |
| **Aircraft Systems Maintenance** | Performs maintenance of aircraft accessory systems, propulsion systems, fabrication of metal and fabric materials used in aircraft structural repair, and inspection and preservation of aircraft parts and materials. | Electrical or mechanical aptitude and manual dexterity. Electronics, mathematics, hydraulics, mechanics, chemistry, metal-working and mechanical drafting desirable. | Aircraft mechanic, aircraft electrician, sheet metal worker, welder, machinist. |
| **Aircrew Operations** | Primary duties require frequent and regular flights. Inflight | High electrical and mechanical aptitude, manual dexterity, | Aircraft mechanic, electrician, hydraulic tester, oxygen systems |

Refueling Operator performs duties associated with inflight refueling of aircraft; Defensive Aerial Gunner is a B-52 integrated crewmember with responsibility for defense of the aircraft; Aircraft Loadmaster supervises loading of cargo and passengers and operates aircraft equipment; Pararescue/ Recovery personnel perform aircrew protection skills; and Flight Engineers ensure mechanical condition of the aircraft and monitor inflight aircraft systems.

normal vision and good physical condition. Mathematics, physics, general science, English, typing, computer principles, and shopwork desirable.

tester, cargo handler, dispatcher and shipping clerk depending upon the area in which training and experience is received. No civilian job covers some aspects of this field.

**Aircrew Protection**

Performs functions involved in the instruction of aircrew and other designated personnel on the principles, procedures, and techniques of global survival. This includes life support equipment, recovery, evasion, captivity, resistance to exploitation and escape.

Good physical condition required; knowledge of pioneering and woodsman activities helpful. Courses in communications, science, and education desirable.

No civilian job covers the scope of the jobs in this career field, but a related job is that of hunting or fishing guide.

**Avionic Systems**

Installs, maintains and repairs airborne bomb navigation, fire control, weapon control, automatic flight control systems, radio and navigation equipment and maintains associated test and precision measurement equipment.

Electronic aptitude, manual dexterity and normal vision. Mathematics, physics, chemistry, electronics and trigonometry desirable.

Radar, television and precision instrument maintenance.

| Career Fields | Duties & Responsibilities | Qualifications | Examples of Civilian Jobs |
|---|---|---|---|
| **Band** | Plays musical instruments in concert bands and orchestras, repairs and maintains instruments, vocalist, performs as drum major, arranges music and maintains music libraries. | Knowledge of rudiments of music, elementary theory of music and orchestration desirable. | Orchestrator, music librarian, music teacher, instrumental musician. |
| **Command Control Systems Operations** | Performs functions involved in aerospace surveillance and aerospace vehicle detection, including missile warning systems, controlling, and plotting. Includes control tower and airways operation; ground-controlled approach procedures; operation of all types of ground radar and related communications equipment, except weather equipment. | Good physical and emotional condition required. Courses in typing, mathematics, business machines, communication, English, and science desirable. | |
| **Communication- Electronics Systems** | Installs, modifies, maintains, repairs and overhauls airborne and ground television equipment, high speed general and special purpose data processing equipment, automatic communications and cryptographic machines systems, teletypewriter, teleautographic equipment, telecommunications systems control and associated electronic test equipment. | Basic knowledge of electronic theory. Mathematics and physics desirable. Normal color vision mandatory. | Communications, electronics technician, radio and television repairer, meteorological and teletype equipment repairer. |

| | | | |
|---|---|---|---|
| **Control Systems Operations** | Operates control towers, directs aircraft landings with radar landing control equipment; operates ground radar equipment, aircraft control centers, airborne radar equipment, space tracking and missile warning systems. | Equipment dexterity, clear voice and speech ability and excellent vision. English desirable. | Aircraft log clerk, airport control operator and air traffic controller. |
| **Dental** | Operates dental facilities and provides paraprofessional dental care; preventive dental services, treatment of oral tissues and fabricates prosthetic devices. | Knowledge of oral and dental anatomy; biology and chemistry desirable. | Dental hygienist, dental assistant. |
| **Education and Training** | Conducts formal classes of instruction, uses training aids, develops material for various courses of instruction; teaches classes in general academic subjects and military matters, and administers educational programs. | English composition and speech desirable. | Vocational training instructor, counselor, educational consultant, or administrator. |
| **Fire Protection** | Operates fire fighting equipment, prevents and extinguishes aircraft and structural fires; rescues and renders first aid; maintains fire fighting and fire prevention equipment. | Good physical condition, no allergies to oil and fire extinguishing solutions; general science and chemistry desirable. | Fire chief, fire extinguisher service person, fire fighter, fire marshal and fire department person. |
| **Fuels** | Receives, stores, dispenses, tests and inspects propellants, petroleum fuels and products. | Chemistry, math, and general science desirable. | Petroleum industry supervisor and bulk plant manager. |
| **Geodetic** | Procures, compiles, computes and uses topographic, | Ability to use precision instruments required in measuring | Cartographer, topographical drafter, mapmaker, and |

109

| Career Fields | Duties & Responsibilities | Qualifications | Examples of Civilian Jobs |
|---|---|---|---|
| | photogrammetric, and cartographic data in preparing aeronautical charts, topographic maps and target folders. | and drafting; algebra, geometry, trigonometry and physics necessary. | advertising layout person. |
| Information Systems Operator | Operates radio and wire communications systems, automatic digital switching equipment, cryptographic devices, airborne and ground electronic countermeasures equipment, all kinds of communication equipment, and the management of radio frequencies. Collects, processes, records, prepares and submits data for various automated systems, analyzes design, programs and operates computer systems. | Knowledge of telecommunications functions and operations of electronic communications equipment. Typing or keyboard experience, and clear speaking voice desirable in many specialties. Business math, algebra and geometry desirable. | Central office operator (telephone and telegraph), cryptographer, radio operator, telephone supervisor and photo-radio operator. Card-tape converter or computer operator, data typist, data processing control clerk, high-speed printer operator, programmer. |
| Intelligence | Collects, produces and disseminates data of strategic, tactical or technical value from an intelligence viewpoint. Maintains information security. | Knowledge of techniques of evaluation, and analysis, interpretation and reporting, foreign languages, English composition, photography, mathematics and typing desirable. | Cryptoanalyst, drafts person, interpreter, investigator, statistician, radio operator and translator. |
| Intricate Equipment Maintenance | Overhauls and modifies photographic equipment; work with fine precision tools, testing devices and schematic drawings. | Considerable mechanical ability and manual dexterity; algebra and physics desirable. Must have normal color vision. | Camera repairer, statistical machine and medical equipment service person. |

| Category | Duties | Qualifications | Civilian Counterparts |
|---|---|---|---|
| **Legal** | Takes and transcribes verbal recordings of legal proceedings, uses stenomask; performs office administrative tasks; processes claims. | Knowledge of stenomask, typewriter, legal terminology, military processing of claims; English grammar and composition; ability to speak clearly and distinctly. | Law librarian, court clerk and shorthand reporter. |
| **Management Analysis** | Collects, processes, records, controls, analyzes, and interprets special and recurring reports, statistical data and other information. | Knowledge of business statistics, mathematics, accounting and English desirable. Completion of high school or GED equivalent mandatory. | Statistical, accounting and budget clerk. |
| **Mechanical/ Electrical** | Performs installation, operation, maintenance and repairs of base direct support systems and equipment. | Physics, mathematics, blueprint reading and electricity. | Elevator repairer, electrician, lineman, powerhouse repairer, diesel mechanic, pipefitter, steamfitter and heating and ventilating worker. |
| **Medical** | Operates medical facilities, works with professional medical staff as they provide care and treatment. May specialize in such medical services as nuclear medicine, cardiopulmonary techniques, physical and occupational therapy, orthopedic appliances, medical laboratory and medical administrative services. | Knowledge of first aid, ability to help professional medical personnel; anatomy, biology, zoology. High school algebra and chemistry desirable in most specialties and are mandatory requirements for some. | X-ray and medical record technician, medical laboratory and pharmacist assistant. Respiratory therapy technician and surgical technologist. |
| **Missile Systems Maintenance** | Assemble, transport, install, maintain, inspect, modify, check out and repair missiles, missile airframes and subsystems and remotely piloted vehicles. | Mechanical or electrical aptitude and manual dexterity. Mathematics and physics desirable. Normal color vision mandatory. | Missile facilities repairer, electronics mechanic, and aircraft mechanical/electrical system repairer. Mechanical inspector, mechanical engineer, aircraft |

| Career Fields | Duties & Responsibilities | Qualifications | Examples of Civilian Jobs |
|---|---|---|---|
| | Inspects, maintains, repairs, calibrates, and modifies missile facilities support systems, liquid propellant systems, test equipment, and related missile and remotely piloted vehicle subsystems. | | mechanic and pneumatic tester and mechanic. |
| Missile Maintenance | Performs missile engine installation, maintenance and repair; maintenance, repair and modification of missile airframes, subsystems and associated aerospace ground equipment. | Mechanical aptitude and manual dexterity. Mathematics and physics desirable. Normal color vision mandatory. | Mechanical inspector, mechanical engineer, aircraft mechanic, and pneumatic tester and mechanic. |
| Morale, Welfare and Recreation | Conducts physical conditioning, coaches sports programs, administers recreation, entertainment, sports and club activities. | Good muscular coordination; English, business math and physical education desirable. | Athletic or playground director, physical education instructor and manager of a recreational establishment. |
| Motor Vehicle Maintenance | Overhauls and maintains powered ground vehicles and mechanical equipment for transporting personnel and supplies. | Machine shop, mathematics and training in the use of tools and blueprints helpful. | Automobile accessories installer, automobile repairer, bus mechanic, carburetor person, automotive electrician and truck mechanic. |
| Munitions and Weapons Maintenance | Maintains and repairs aircraft armament; assembles, maintains, loads, unloads and stores munitions and nuclear weapons; disposes of bombs, missiles and rockets and operates detection instruments. | Mechanical or electrical aptitude, manual dexterity, normal color vision and depth perception. Mathematics, mechanics, and physics desirable. | Aircraft armament mechanic, armorer, ammunition inspector, munitions handler. |

| | | | |
|---|---|---|---|
| **Personnel** | Interviews, classifies, selects career jobs for airmen on the basis of qualifications and requirements of the Air Force; administers aptitude, performance tests; administers personnel quality control programs; performs counseling, educational and administrative functions. | English composition and speech. Operation of simple data processing equipment and typing ability desirable. | Employment or personnel clerk, special service supervisor, personnel service manager, personnel supervisor, counselor. |
| **Public Affairs** | Interviews people; reports news; composes, proofreads, writes and edits news copy; provides public affairs advice. | High general aptitude and completion of high school or GED equivalency mandatory. English grammar and composition, speech, journalism, drama, radio/television, history, or political science desirable. | Reporter, copy reader, historian, public relations representative, editorial assistant, broadcast or program director, announcer. |
| **Reprographic** | Operates and maintains reproduction equipment used in the graphic arts, performs hand and machine composition and binding operations. | Mechanical ability and dexterity; courses in chemistry and shop mechanics desirable. | Lithographic press, fold machine, offset and webpress, perforating machine or duplicating machine operator; bookbinder; photolithographer; photoengraver. |
| **Safety** | Performs functions related to the conduct of both safety and disaster preparedness programs. Conducts safety programs, surveys areas and activities to eliminate hazards, analyzes accident causes and trends. Trains personnel to accomplish the primary mission under the handicaps imposed by | Knowledge of industrial hygiene, safety education, safety psychology, and blueprint interpretation. Typing, English, public speaking, mathematics, and science desirable. | Safety inspector and instructor. |

| Career Fields | Duties & Responsibilities | Qualifications | Examples of Civilian Jobs |
|---|---|---|---|
| | enemy attack and by acts of man and nature. | | |
| Sanitation | Operates and maintains water and waste processing plant systems and equipment and performs pest and rodent control functions. | Physics, biology, chemistry and blueprint reading valuable. | Purification plant operator, sanitary inspector, exterminator and entomologist. |
| Security Police | Provide security for classified information and material, enforce law and order, control traffic, and protect lives and property, organize as local ground defense forces. | Good physical condition, vision and hearing; civics and social sciences desirable. | Guard, police inspector, police officer, and superintendent of police. |
| Special Investigations/ Counterintelligence | Investigates violations of the Uniform Code of Military Justice and applicable federal statues, investigates conditions pertaining to sabotage, espionage, treason, sedition and security. | Knowledge of law enforcement and security regulations, good physical condition, hearing and vision; civics, social sciences, accounting and foreign language desirable. | Detective, chief of detectives, detective sergeant and investigator. |
| Structural/ Pavements | Constructs and maintains structural facilities and pavement area; maintains pavements, railroads and soil bases; performs erosion control; operates heavy equipment; performs site development, general maintenance, cost and real property accounting, work control functions and metal fabricating. | Blueprint reading, mechanical drawing, mathematics, physics, and chemistry. | Plumber, bricklayer, carpenter, stonemason, painter, construction work, welder and sheet metal worker. |

| Career Field | Description | Requirements | Related Civilian Occupations |
|---|---|---|---|
| **Supply** | Designs, develops, analyzes and operates supply data systems including supply data systems; responsible for computation, operation and management of material facilities; equipment review and validation; records maintenance, inventory and distribution control; budget computation and financial plans. | Accounting and business administration. | Junior accountant, machine records section supervisor, receiving, shipping and stock clerk. |
| **Services and Food Services** | Supervises and operates sales stores, laundry/dry cleaning facilities, commissaries and meat processing. Cooks and bakes. | Chemistry, management, marketing, manual dexterity and business mathematics. | Department manager, retail general merchandise manager, meat cutter, butcher, chef and pastry cook. |
| **Training Devices** | Installs, maintains, repairs, modifies and operates training devices such as cockpit procedures trainers, flight and mission trainers and simulators, navigation and tactics training devices, visual training devices, missile crew procedures trainers, and offensive and defensive systems trainers. | Knowledge of electricity, mathematics, blueprint reading and physics desirable. | Link trainer, instructor, radio mechanic. |
| **Transportation** | Ensures service, efficiency and economy of transportation of supplies and personnel by aircraft, train, motor vehicle and ship. | Driver training, operation of office machines and business math. | Cargo handler, motor vehicle dispatcher, shipping or traffic rate clerk, trailer truck driver and ticket agent. |
| **Visual Information** | Operates aerial and ground cameras, motion picture and other photographic equipment; processes photographs and film, | Considerable dexterity on small precision equipment; excellent eyesight. Mathematics, physics, chemistry, public speaking, | Photographer, darkroom technician, film editor, aerial commercial photographer, photograph finisher, sound mixer |

| Career Fields | Duties & Responsibilities | Qualifications | Examples of Civilian Jobs |
|---|---|---|---|
| | edits motion pictures, performs photographic instrumentation functions, and operates airborne, field and precision processing laboratories. | commercial art, drafting, photography, drama, communicative arts, and computer science desirable. | and motion picture camera operator. |
| Wire Communications Systems Maintenance | Installs and maintains wire communications equipment and systems. Installs, repairs and maintains telephone and telegraph land line systems, telephone equipment, antenna support systems, key systems, telephone switching equipment, missile communications control systems and electronic switching equipment. | Mechanical/electronic aptitude and manual dexterity; physics and mathematics desirable. Normal color perception mandatory. Physical ability to climb required in some specialties. | Cable splicer, central office repairer, line installer and inspector, teletype and central office manual equipment repairer. |
| Weather | Collects, records and analyzes meteorological data; makes visual and instrument weather observations. Forecasts immediate and long-range weather conditions. | Visual acuity correctable to 20/20; physics, mathematics and geography desirable. | Meteorologist, weather forecaster and weather observer. |

## National Guard–Related Abbreviations

**AD**   Active Duty. Full-time duty in the military service of the United States, other than active duty for training (ADT).

**ADT**   Active Duty for Training. This duty includes annual training (AT), participation in small arms competition, attendance at military conferences, short tours for special projects, ferrying of aircraft, and participation in command post exercises (CPX) and field maneuvers.

**AFQT**   Armed Forces Qualification Test.

**AFSC**   Air Force Specialty Code (Air Force Military Occupational Specialty).

**AG**   Adjutant General.

**AGR**   Active (duty) Guard/Reserve. All active duty performed by reserve component personnel in excess of 179 consecutive days, in connection with organizing, administering, recruiting, instructing, or training the reserve components.

**AIT**   Advanced Individual Training.

**ANG**   Air National Guard.

**ARNG**   Army National Guard.

**ASVAB**   Armed Services Vocational Aptitude Battery.

**AT**   Annual Training. Period of Full-Time Training Duty (FTTD) for members of the Army and Air National Guard, usually 15 days a year.

**BAQ**   Basic Allowance for Quarters (for FTTD, ADT, and AD only).

**BAS**   Basic Allowance for Subsistence (for FTTD, ADT, and AD only).

**BAT**   Basic Aptitudes Test.

**BCT**   Basic Combat Training.

**BT**   Basic Training (initial active duty training for Army Guard).

BMT   Basic Military Training (initial active duty training for Air Guard).

DOR   Date of Rank (effective date of last promotion).
DOPMA   Defense Officer Personnel Management Act.

EAD   Entry on Active Duty, extended active duty.
EEO   Equal Employment Opportunity. Programs that implement Title VII of the Civil Rights Act of 1964 as amended by PL 92-261, for civil service employees of the federal government, including National Guard technicians.
EFMP   Enlisted Force Management Plan.
EPMS   Enlisted Personnel Management System.
ET   Equivalent Training (making up a drill period missed for some legitimate reason).
ETS   Expiration Term of Service (date military obligation is completed).

FICA   Federal Insurance Contributions Act (Social Security pay deduction).
FTM   Additional Full-Time Manning. High priority units are authorized extra personnel to help meet requirements. May be active or Guard.
FTRF   Full-time Recruiter Force (Guardsmen on active duty tours for recruiting duty).
FTTD   Full-time Training Duty. Performed in states under Title 32 USC while in attendance at Army service schools.
FY   Fiscal Year (federal fiscal years run from October 1 to September 30 annually).

GED   General Educational Development (equivalent of high school diploma).
GS   General Schedule (Civil Service civilian employees), also Guard technicians.

HR/EO   Human Relations/Equal Opportunity. Efforts by the ARNG to eliminate prejudice and discrimination toward racial and ethnic minorities and women, promote harmony, and develop attitudes that support unit teamwork/equal consideration based on merit, fitness and capability.

IADT/IEF   Initial Active Duty Training/Initial Entry Training. All phases of training before initial award of MOS.

IDT   Inactive Duty Training. Training performed in a federal status while not on active duty—weekend drills, Unit Training Assemblies, etc.

ING   Inactive National Guard. Continuing military status for Guardsmen temporarily unable to participate in regular IDT.

IRR   Individual Ready Reserve.

JUMPS   Joint Uniform Military Pay System.

KPUP   Key Personnel Upgrade Program.

MEPS   Military Entrance Processing Station.

MOS   Military Occupational Specialty (an Army Guardsman's specific military skill).

MUTA   Multiple Unit Training Assembly.

NG   National Guard.

NGB   National Guard Bureau.

NPS   Non-prior Service enlistee (enlistee with no active duty service).

OBV   Obligated Volunteer Officer (officer who has not completed military obligation).

OER   Officer Evaluation Report, Officer Effectiveness Report.

OPMS    Officer Personnel Management System.
OSB    Officer Selection Battery.
OSUT    One-Station Unit Training.

PEBD    Pay Entry Basic Date (date military service began for pay purposes).
PL    Public Law.
PMOS    Primary Military Occupational Specialty.
PS    Prior Service enlistee (served previously on active duty).

REFRAD    Release from Active Duty.
ROPA    Reserve Officer Personnel Act.
ROPMA    Reserve Officer Personnel Management Act.
ROTC    Reserve Officers Training Corps.
RYE    Retirement Year Ending. End of the 12-month period in which a Guardsman serving in an active drill status must earn a minimum of 50 inactive duty training (IDT) points to be credited with a satisfactory year for Reserve retirement credit.

SAD    State Active Duty (Guard units ordered to state service).
SBP    Survivor Benefit Plan.
SGLI    Servicemen's Group Life Insurance.
SMOS    Secondary Military Occupational Specialty.
SMP    Simultaneous Membership Program (member of Army Guard and college-level Army Reserve Officers Training Corps (ROTC) at the same time).
SQT    Skill Qualification Test.
STARC    State Area Command.
SUTA    Split-Unit Training Assembly.

TA    Table of Allowances.

TDA   Table of Distribution and Allowances (MTDA—Modified TDA).

TOE   Table of Organization and Equipment (MTOE—Modified TOE).

TDY   Temporary Duty.

TECH   Technician. Full-time career civilian employee of the National Guard, normally a military member of the unit for which employed, who provides day-to-day continuity of the military unit's operations.

USAFR   United States Air Force Reserve.

USAR   United States Army Reserve.

USC   United States Code.

USPFO   United States Property and Fiscal Officer.

UTA   Unit Training Assembly (inactive duty training period of at least 4 hours' duration).

WOCS   Warrant Officer Candidate School.

### Phonetic Alphabet

The phonetic alphabet is used by the National Guard and all the military services. It is used in radio communications, telephonic messages, and oral communications to avoid misunderstandings in transmitting messages.

| | | | |
|---|---|---|---|
| A | ALFA | I | INDIA |
| B | BRAVO | J | JULIET |
| C | CHARLIE | K | KILO |
| D | DELTA | L | LIMA |
| E | ECHO | M | MIKE |
| F | FOXTROT | N | NOVEMBER |
| G | GOLF | O | OSCAR |
| H | HOTEL | P | PAPA |

| Q | QUEBEC | V | VICTOR |
|---|--------|---|--------|
| R | ROMEO | W | WHISKEY |
| S | SIERRA | X | XRAY |
| T | TANGO | Y | YANKEE |
| U | UNIFORM | Z | ZULU |

## Military Time

All the military runs on military time. Hours of the day are numbered from 1 to 24. In the afternoon, instead of starting again with 1, the military goes on to 13. The hours 8 a.m. and 7 p.m. are called 0800 (zero eight hundred) and 1900 (nineteen hundred). Never say "nineteen hundred hours." For hours and minutes, 10:45 a.m. is 1045 (ten forty-five); 9:30 p.m. is 2130 (twenty-one thirty).

Inside represents a.m.
Outside represents p.m.

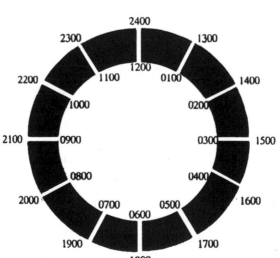

## Code of Conduct

The Code of Conduct is a creed by which all military members must serve. It applies to all services at all times, in both peace and war. You will probably have to memorize the code in basic training. It consists of six articles:

Article I

I am an American fighting man. I serve in the forces which guard my country and our way of life. I am prepared to give my life in their defense.

Article II

I will never surrender of my own free will. If in command I will never surrender my men while they still have the means to resist.

Article III

If I am captured, I will continue to resist by all means available. I will make every effort to escape and aid others to escape. I will accept neither parole nor special favors from the enemy.

Article IV

If I become a prisoner of war, I will keep faith with my fellow prisoners. I will give no information or take part in any action which might be harmful to my comrades. If I am senior, I will take command. If not, I will obey the lawful orders of those appointed over me and will back them up in every way.

Article V

When questioned, should I become a prisoner of war, I am required to give only name, rank, service number, and date of birth. I will evade answering further questions to the utmost of my ability. I will make no oral or written statements disloyal to my country and its allies or harmful to their cause.

Article VI
I will never forget that I am an American fighting man, responsible for my actions, and dedicated to the principles which make my country free. I will trust in God and in the United States of America.

### Eleven General Orders

The eleven General Orders are common to all branches of the armed forces. You will have to learn them in basic training and stay familiar with them all the time you are in the Guard. The orders are modified slightly by each service for its own use.

1. To take charge of my post and all government property in view.
2. To stand my post in a military manner, keeping always on the alert and observing everything that takes place within sight or hearing.
3. To report all violations of order I am instructed to enforce.
4. To report all alarms, calls for assistance, and safety hazards to the Officer of the Day.
5. To quit my post only when properly relieved.
6. To receive, obey, and pass on to my relief all orders from the Commanding Officer, Officer of the Day, and officers and non-commissioned officers of the guard section.
7. To talk to no one except in the line of duty.
8. To give alarm in case of fire or disorder.
9. To call the Duty Non-Commissioned Officer in any case not covered by instructions.

10. To salute all officers and all colors and standards not cased. (Colors and standards refer to US flags.)
11. To be especially watchful at night and to allow no one to pass without proper authority.

### Job Rights for Members of the National Guard

You may have some concerns about the effect of your membership in the National Guard on your civilian employment. Fortunately, the rights of members of the Guard as well as the rights of rights of employers are spelled out by law. The rights of an Army or Air Guardsman to participate in weekend drills and annual training are clearly defined and specified under federal law. Listed below are several answers to key questions concerning job rights for both employee and employer.

Q.  Is an employer required to excuse a worker for military training duty?

A.  Yes. Chapter 43 of Part III of Title 38, US Code, places responsibilities on the employee and the employer; one must go and the other must let him.

Q.  May an employer discharge an employee because of his reserve membership or his participation in reserve activities?

A.  No.

Q.  How about an employee's pay for time lost from work because of military training?

A.  Employers are not required to pay for lost time because of training. Some do as a matter of policy or contract; others do not.

Q.  Are any employment rights or benefits protected by law?

A.   Yes. The employee cannot be denied promotion or any other benefits or advantages of employment because of his reserve obligation.

Q.   Are all employees in all kinds of employment covered by this federal law?

A.   Yes, except for those who hold temporary positions. Coverage now extends not only to employees in private industry and the federal government, but also to employees who work for state and local governments.

Q.   What is the employee's responsibility?

A.   He should return to work as soon as his training has ended.

Q.   May the employer demand to know exactly when the employee will return?

A.   No. It is reasonable to want this information but sometimes impossible for the trainee to furnish. The law states that the trainee should report for work following training at the beginning of his next regularly scheduled working period after the end of the last day necessary for him to travel from the place of training to his place of employment, or within a reasonable time thereafter if he is delayed by factors beyond his control.

Q.   Does the branch of service make any difference?

A.   No. Job protection extends alike to members of all branches of service and to all kinds of military training.

Q.   Is the employee required to inform his employer?

A.   Yes. He must request leave for the training period. No particular form is required. When you are told of your training dates, you should in turn tell your employer. In effect, you request leave to participate in the training.

Q.   May the employer deny the request?

A.   No. The law requires the employer to grant leave.

Q.   How about vacation time? Can the military leave be charged against it?

A.   No. Whatever vacation rights an employee has, he keeps without loss because of training time.

Q.   Will an employee who has accrued paid vacation time of so many days when he begins his training still have the same amount of time when he returns?

A.   Yes.

Q.   Suppose there is no regular shift or schedule of work, as in the case of a sales worker?

A.   Since reporting for work is the normal way of ending leave of all kinds, it is enough and appropriate that the employee notify the employer and begin work on the day that would be his normal workday.

Q.   Does the trainee lose his right to return to work if he delays reporting beyond the time prescribed under the law?

A.   No. But he will be subject to the conduct rules of the employer pertaining to explanations and discipline with respect to absence from scheduled work.

Q.   Is a formal application for reemployment required?

A.   No. An employee on leave for training is not "out of work" in the sense that he is "reemployed" on his return. It is more correct to say that he simply returns to his job.

Q.   What if an employee is disabled during training and is unable to return to his job.

A. In most cases disability extends the length of time an employee is allowed to return to work. Where the disability turns out to handicap the employee over an extended period of time, there are still employer responsibilities. Each case should be reviewed with a representative of the Labor Department's Office of Veteran Reemployment Rights.

Q. If I encounter problems with my employer with regard to my attendance at military training, what is the first step in resolving the problem?

A. In most cases the problem can be resolved by your unit First Sergeant or Commander through a phone call. Perhaps it may require a visit to your employer by a representative of your unit. However, be assured that unit personnel are there to assist you with problems.

### Federally Operated Military Installations
### (Including those utilized by Guardsmen for MOS/AFSC qualification, and Annual Training)

**ALABAMA**
Anniston Army Depot, 36201
Fort McClellan, 36201
Fort Rucker, 36362
Gunter AFS, 36114
Maxwell AFB, 36112
Redstone Arsenal, 35809
**ALASKA**
Eielson AFB, 99702
Elmendorf AFB, 99506
Fort Greely, 98733
Fort Richardson, 98731
Fort Wainwright, 98731
Shemya AFB, 98736
**ARIZONA**
Davis-Monthan AFB, 85707
Florence Military Reservation,

85232
Fort Huachuca, 85613
Luke AFB, 85309
Navajo Depot, Flagstaff 86002
Williams AFB, 85224
Yuma Proving Grounds, 85364
**ARKANSAS**
Blytheville AFB, 72315
Fort Chaffee, 72318
Little Rock AFB, 72076
Pine Bluff Arsenal, 71601
**CALIFORNIA**
Beale AFB, 95903
Castle AFB, 95342
Edwards AFB, 93523
Fort Irwin, 92311
Ford Ord, 93941

Presidio of
 San Francisco, 94129
George AFB, 92393
Los Angeles AFS, 90009
March AFB, 92518
Mather AFB, 95655
McClellan AFB, 95652
Norton AFB, 92409
Oakland Army Base, 94614
Sacramento Army
 Depot, 95330
Sierra Army Depot, 96113
Travis AFB, 94535
Vandenberg AFB, 93437
**COLORADO**
Fitzsimons Gen. Hosp. 80240
Fort Carson, 80913
Lowry AFB, 80230
Peterson AFB, 80914
Pueblo Army Depot, 81002
U.S. Air Force Academy, 80840
**DELAWARE**
Dover AFB, 19901
**DISTRICT OF COLUMBIA**
Bolling AFB, 20332
Fort McNair, 20315
**FLORIDA**
Eglin AFB, 32542
Homestead AFB, 33039
Hurlburt Field, 32544
MacDill AFB, 33608
Patrick AFB, 32935
Tyndall AFB, 32403
**GEORGIA**
Atlanta Army Depot, 30050
Dobbins AFB, 30060
Fort Benning, 31905
Fort Gordon, 30905
Fort McPherson, 30330
Fort Stewart, 31313
Moody AFB, 31601
Robins AFB, 31098
**HAWAII**
Bellows AFS, 96553
Fort Shafter Mil Res, 96558

Hickam AFB, 96853
Schofield Barracks, APO 96557
Wheeler AFB, 96854
**IDAHO**
Mountain Home AFB, 83648
**ILLINOIS**
Chanute AFB, 61868
Fort Sheridan, 60037
Marseilles Training Area 61341
O'Hare Intl Aprt, 60666
Rock Island Arsenal, 61202
Scott AFB, 62225
**INDIANA**
Fort Benjamin Harrison, 46216
Grissom AFB, 46971
**KANSAS**
Fort Leavenworth, 66027
Ft. Riley, 66442
McConnell AFB, 67221
Nickell Barracks, Salina 67402
**KENTUCKY**
Winchester Eastern Tng Site 40391
Fort Campbell, 42223
Fort Knox, 40121
**LOUISIANA**
Barksdale AFB, 71110
England AFB, 71301
Fort Polk, 71459
New Orleans NAS, 70146
**MAINE**
Loring AFB, 04751
**MARYLAND**
Aberdeen Proving Ground, 21005
Andrews AFB, 20331
Fort Detrick, 21701
Fort Meade, 20755
Fort Ritchie, 21719
**MASSACHUSETTS**
Camp Edwards
Fort Devens, 01433
L.G. Hanscom AFB, 01731
Westover AFB, 01022
**MICHIGAN**
K.I. Sawyer AFB, 49843
Wurtsmith AFB, 48753

**MINNESOTA**
Minn-St. Paul Intl Aprt, 55450
**MISSISSIPPI**
Columbus AFB, 39701
Keesler AFB, 39534
**MISSOURI**
Fort Leonard Wood, 65473
Richards-Gebaur AFB, 64030
Whiteman AFB, 65301
**MONTANA**
Malmstrom AFB, 59402
**NEBRASKA**
Offutt AFB, 68113
**NEVADA**
Nellis AFB, 89191
**NEW HAMPSHIRE**
Pease AFB, 03801
**NEW JERSEY**
Fort Dix, 06840
Fort Monmouth, 07703
McGuire AFB, 08641
**NEW MEXICO**
Cannon AFB, 88101
Holloman AFB, 88330
Kirtland AFB, 87117
White Sands Missile Range, 88002
**NEW YORK**
Fort Drum, 13603
Fort Hamilton, 11252
Griffiss AFB, 13441
Niagara Falls Intl Aprt, 14304
Plattsburgh AFB, 12903
Seneca Army Depot, 14541
**NORTH CAROLINA**
Fort Bragg, 28307
Pope AFB, 28309
Seymour Johnson AFB, 27531
**NORTH DAKOTA**
Grand Forks AFB, 58205
Minot AFB, 58705
**OHIO**
Wright-Patterson AFB, 45433
Youngstown Muni Aprt, 44473
**OKLAHOMA**
Altus AFB, 73521

Fort Sill, 73503
Tinker AFB, 73145
Vance AFB, 73701
**PENNSYLVANIA**
Carlisle Barracks, 17013
Fort Indiantown Gap, 17003
Letterkenny Army Depot, 17201
New Cumberland Army Depot,
  17070
Pittsburgh Intl Aprt, 15231
Tobyhanna Army Depot, 18502
Willow Grove Air Res. Fac.,
  19090
**PUERTO RICO**
Fort Buchanan, 00934
**SOUTH CAROLINA**
Charleston AFB, 29404
Fort Jackson, 29207
Myrtle Beach AFB, 29577
Shaw AFB, 29152
**SOUTH DAKOTA**
Ellsworth AFB, 57706
**TENNESSEE**
Arnold AFS, 37389
**TEXAS**
Bergstrom AFB, 78743
Brooks AFB, 78235
Carswell AFB, 76127
Dyess AFB, 79607
Fort Bliss, 79906
Fort Hood, 76544
Fort Sam Houston, 78234
Goodfellow AFB, 76903
Kelly AFB, 78241
Lackland AFB, 78236
Laughlin AFB, 78840
Randolph AFB, 78148
Red River Army Depot, 75501
Reese AFB, 79489
Sheppard AFB, 76331
**UTAH**
Dugway Proving Grounds, 84022
Fort Douglas, 84113
Hill AFB, 84056
Tooele Army Depot, 84075

**VERMONT**
Underhill Range, 05489
**VIRGINIA**
Fort A.P. Hill, 23150
Fort Belvoir, 22060
Fort Eustis, 26304
Fort Lee, 23801
Fort Monroe, 23351
Fort Myer, 22211
Fort Pickett, 23824
Fort Story, 23459

Langley AFB, 23665
**WASHINGTON**
Fairchild AFB, 99011
Fort Lewis, 98433
McChord AFB, 98438
Yakima Firing Range, 98901
**WISCONSIN**
Camp Douglas, 54618
Fort McCoy, 54656
**WYOMING**
F.E. Warren AFB, 82201

## State-owned Training Installations Army Guard

**ARIZONA**
Phoenix (Papago Park), 85008
**ARKANSAS**
Camp Robinson (No. Little Rock),
  72115
**CALIFORNIA**
Camp San Luis Obispo, 93401 '
**COLORADO**
Camp George West (Golden),
  80401
**CONNECTICUT**
Camp Hartell (Windsor Locks),
  06096
Camp O'Neill (Niantic) 06357
Stone's Ranch (E. Lyme), 06333
**DELAWARE**
Bethany Beach (Rehoboth), 19930
**FLORIDA**
Camp Blanding (Starke), 32901
**ILLINOIS**
Camp Lincoln (Springfield), 62706
**IOWA**
Camp Dodge (Des Moines), 50303
**LOUISIANA**
Camp Beauregard (Pineville),
  71360
Camp Villere (Slidell), 70458
Jackson Barracks
  (New Orleans), 70146

**MAINE**
Camp Keyes (Augusta), 04330
Hollis Plains (Buxton) 64042
**MARYLAND**
Gunpowder Target Range
  (Glen Arm), 21057
State Mil Res (Havre de Grace),
  21078
**MASSACHUSETTS**
Camp Curtis Guild (Wakefield),
  01880
**MICHIGAN**
Camp Grayling (Grayling), 49738
**MINNESOTA**
Camp Ripley (Little Falls), 56345
**MISSISSIPPI**
Camp Shelby (Hattiesburg), 39401
**NEW HAMPSHIRE**
Camp La Bonte, SMR (Concord),
  03301
**NEW JERSEY**
Sea Girt, 08750
**NEW YORK**
Camp Smith (Peekskill), 10567
**NORTH CAROLINA**
Camp Butner (Butner), 27509
**NORTH DAKOTA**
Camp G.C. Graften (Devils Lake),
  58301

**OHIO**
Camp Perry (Port Clinton), 43452
**OREGON**
Camp Rilea (Astoria), 97103
Camp Withycombe
(Clackamas), 97015
**RHODE ISLAND**
Camp Varum (Narragansett),
02882
**SOUTH DAKOTA**
Camp Rapid (Rapid City), 47704
**TEXAS**
Camp Barkeley (Abilene), 79605
Camp Bowie (Brownwood), 76801
Camp Mabry (Austin), 78703

Camp Maxey (Parish), 75460
Eagle Mt. Lake (Newark) 76071
**UTAH**
Camp W.G. Williams (Lehi),
84065
**VERMONT**
Camp Johnson (Burlington) 05404
**VIRGINIA**
State Mil. Res. (Va. Beach), 23451
**WEST VIRGINIA**
Camp Dawson (Kingwood), 26537
**WISCONSIN**
Camp Williams (Tomash) 54616
**WYOMING**
Camp Guernsey (Guernsey), 82001

## Federally Owned, State-operated Training Installations—Army Guard

**ALASKA**
Camp Carroll (Anchorage), 98731
**ARIZONA**
Buckeye Range (Buckeye)
**CALIFORNIA**
Camp Roberts (Paso Robles),
83451
Los Alamitos AFRC (Los
Alamitos), 94501
**DELAWARE**
New Castle Rifle Range, 19720
**IDAHO**
Gooding Range (Gooding)
Gowan Field (Boise)
Hailey Range (Hailey)
Pocatello Trng Site (Pocatello)
Kimama Trng Site (Rupert)
**INDIANA**
Camp Atterbury-ARFTA
(Edinburg), 46124
**LOUISIANA**
Camp Livingston (Pineville), 71360
New Iberia Trng Site (New Iberia)
**MAINE**
Auburn Range (Auburn)

Caswell Range (Craibou)
Riley-Bog Brook Trng. Site
(Bethel) 04217
**MASSACHUSETTS**
Camp Edwards (Bourne), 01725
**MICHIGAN**
Custer Res For Trng Area (Battle
Creek), 49012
**MISSISSIPPI**
Camp McCain (Grenada), 38901
**MISSOURI**
Camp Clark (Nevada), 64772
Fort Crowder (Neosho), 64850
**MONTANA**
Fort Wm. H. Harrison (Helena),
59601
**NEBRASKA**
Camp Ashland (Ashland), 68003
**NEVADA**
Stead Trng Fac (Reno), 89502
**NEW MEXICO**
Deming Range (Deming)
Tucumcari Range (Tucumcari)
**OKLAHOMA**
Camp Gruber (Muskogee), 74423

**OREGON**
Camp Adair (Corvallis), 97330
**PUERTO RICO**
Camp Santiago (Salinas), 00751
**SOUTH CAROLINA**
Clark Hill Trng. Site (McCormick) 29835
South Carolina Trng. Ctr. (Leesburg) 29290
**TENNESSEE**
Smyrna (Former Stewart AFB), 37167
Catoosa Range, GA (Ft. Oglethorpe), 37204
John Sevier Range (Fountain City)
Milan Arsenal (Lavinia) 38348

**TEXAS**
Camp Swift (Bastrop), 78602
Fort Wolters (Mineral Wells), 78421
**VERMONT**
Ethan Allen (Jericno)
**WASHINGTON**
Camp 7 Mile (Racine)
**WISCONSIN**
Racine County Range (Racine)
**WYOMING**
Lander Range (Lander)
Lovell Range (Lovell)
Sheridan Range (Sheridan)

## Air National Guard Training Sites

**GEORGIA**
Air National Guard Field Trng Site
P. O. Box 7299
Garden City, Georgia, 31402
**MICHIGAN**
Training Site Detachment
Michigan ANG
Phelps-Collins ANGB
Alpena, Michigan, 49707
**MISSISSIPPI**
Headquarters Air National Guard Training Site
Mississippi ANG

P.O. Box 1300
Gulfport, Mississippi, 39501
**TENNESSEE**
IG Brown ANG
Professional Military Education Center (PMEC)
Knoxville, Tennessee 37901
**WISCONSIN**
Air National Guard Permanent Training Site
Volk Field
Camp Douglas, Wisconsin 54618

## Major Army National Guard Units Divisions

26th Infantry Division (-), Massachusetts
  1st Brigade, Massachusetts
  3rd Brigade, Massachusetts
  43rd Brigade, Connecticut
28th Infantry Division, Pennsylvania
  55th Brigade, Pennsylvania
  56th Brigade, Pennsylvania
  2nd Brigade, Pennsylvania

*29th Infantry Division (Light)(-), Virginia
  1st Brigade, Virginia
  2nd Brigade, Virginia
  3rd Brigade, Maryland
*35th Infantry Division (-)(Kansas)
  67th Brigade, Nebraska
  69th Brigade, Kansas
  149th Brigade, Kentucky
38th Infantry Division (-), Indiana
  76th Brigade, Indiana
  2nd Brigade, Indiana
  46th Brigade, Michigan
40th Infantry Division (Mechanized), California
  1st Brigade (Mechanized), California
  2nd Brigade (Mechanized), California
  3rd Brigade (Mechanized), California
42nd Infantry Division, New York
  1st Brigade, New York
  2nd Brigade, New York
  *3rd Brigade, New York
47th Infantry Division (-), Minnesota
  1st Brigade, Minnesota
  34th Brigade, Iowa
  66th Brigade, Illinois
49th Armored Division, Texas
  1st Brigade, Texas
  2nd Brigade, Texas
  3rd Brigade, Texas
50th Armored Division (-), New Jersey
  1st Brigade, New Jersey
  2nd Brigade, New Jersey
  86th Brigade, Vermont
* Still undergoing reorganization

## Brigades

27th Infantry Brigade, (Light) (Roundout), New York
29th Infantry Brigade (Separate), Hawaii
30th Infantry Brigade (Mechanized) (Separate), North Carolina
32nd Infantry Brigade (Mechanized) (Separate), Wisconsin
33rd Infantry Brigade (Separate), Illinois
39th Infantry Brigade (Separate), Arkansas
41st Infantry Brigade (Separate), Oregon
45th Infantry Brigade (Separate), Oklahoma
48th Infantry Brigade (Mechanized) (Roundout), Georgia
53rd Infantry Brigade (Separate), Florida

73rd  Infantry Brigade (Separate), Ohio
81st  Infantry Brigade (Mechanized) (Separate), Washington
92nd  Infantry Brigade (Separate), Puerto Rico
218th  Infantry Brigade (Mechanized) (Separate), South Carolina
256th  Infantry Brigade (Mechanized) (Roundout), Louisiana
30th  Armored Brigade (Separate), Tennessee
31st  Armored Brigade (Separate), Alabama
155th  Armored Brigade (Roundout), Mississippi

## Armored Cavalry Regiments

107th  Armored Cavalry Regiment, Ohio
  1st Squadron, 150th ACR, West Virginia
  2nd Squadron, 107th Cavalry Regiment, Ohio
  3rd Squadron, 107th Cavalry Regiment, Ohio
116th  Armored Cavalry Regiment, Idaho
  1st Squadron, 108th ACR, Mississippi
  2nd Squadron, 116th Cavalry Regiment, Idaho
  3rd Squadron, 116th Cavalry Regiment, Oregon
163rd  Armored Cavalry Regiment, Montana
  1st Squadron, 163d Cavalry Regiment, Montana
  2nd Squadron, 163d Cavalry Regiment, Montana
  3rd Squadron, 163d Cavalry Regiment, Texas
278th  Armored Cavalry Regiment, Tennessee
  1st Squadron, 278th Armored Cavalry Regiment, Tennessee
  2nd Squadron, 278th Armored Cavalry Regiment, Tennessee
  3rd Squadron, 278th Armored Cavalry Regiment, Tennessee

## General Officer Headquarters Units

111th  Air Defense Artillery Brigade, HHB, New Mexico
164th  Air Defense Artillery Brigade, HHB, Florida
I Corps Artillery, HHB, Utah
216th  Signal Command, HHC, Delaware
16th  Engineer Brigade (Combat), HHC, Ohio
30th  Engineer Brigade (Construction), HHC, North Carolina
35th  Engineer Brigade (Combat), HHC, Missouri
66th  Aviation HHC, Washington
194th  Engineer Brigade (Corps), HHC, Tennessee
167th  Support Brigade, HHC, Alabama
43rd  Military Police Brigade, HHC, Rhode Island
49th  Military Police Brigade, HHC, California
177th  Military Police Brigade, HHC, Michigan
260th  Military Police Brigade, HHC, Washington, DC
184th  Transportation Brigade, HHC, Mississippi

112th  Medical Brigade, Ohio
175th  Medical Brigade, California
213th  Medical Brigade, Mississippi

Additional Army Guard units, categorized by their type of mission include:

  18  Field Artillery Brigades (HHB)
   1  Infantry Group (Arctic Recon)
  17  Engineer Groups, HHC
   2  Aviation Groups, HHC
  17  Attack Helicopter Battalions
   4  Support Groups, HHC
   9  Area Support Groups, HHC
   3  Medical Groups, HHD
   2  Military Police Groups, HHC
   2  Signal Groups, HHD
   5  Armor Battalions (Separate)
   2  Infantry Battalions (Mechanized) (Separate)
   4  Infantry Battalions (TLAT)
  48  Field Artillery Battalions
  14  Air Defense Artillery Battalions
  47  Engineer Battalions (Combat)
   3  Support Battalions
  16  Signal Battalions
   2  Special Forces Groups
   1  Corps Support Command, HHC
  54  State Area Commands
  18  Rear Area Operations Centers
 154  Battalion Headquarters Units
 734  Separate Companies & Detachment Size Units
  18  Hospitals
   1  Transportation Movement Control Center (TACOM)
 153  TDA Units and Command (State Hqs, CACs, etc.)
   1  Medical Supply and Optical Maintenance Depot (MEDSOM)

## Major Air National Guard Units
## Aerospace Defense Command

102nd  Fighter Interceptor Wing, Otis ANGB, Massachusetts
120th  Fighter Interceptor Group, Great Falls, Montana
177th  Fighter Interceptor Group, Atlantic City, New Jersey
125th  Fighter Interceptor Group, Jacksonville, Florida
107th  Fighter Interceptor Group, Niagara Falls, New York
142nd  Fighter Interceptor Group, Portland, Oregon
147th  Fighter Interceptor Group, Ellington Field AGS, Texas

191st  Fighter Interceptor Group, Selfridge ANGB, Michigan
144th  Fighter Interceptor Wing, Fresno, California
119th  Fighter Interceptor Group, Fargo, North Dakota
148th  Fighter Interceptor Group, Duluth, Minnesota

## Military Airlift Command

118th  Tactical Airlift Wing, Nashville, Tennessee
133rd  Tactical Airlift Wing, Minneapolis/St. Paul, Minnesota
136th  Tactical Airlift Wing, Dallas NAS, Texas
137th  Tactical Airlift Wing, Will Rogers, Oklahoma
146th  Tactical Airlift Wing, Van Nuys, California
109th  Tactical Airlift Group, Schenectady, New York
130th  Tactical Airlift Group, Charleston, West Virginia
135th  Tactical Airlift Group, Baltimore, Maryland
139th  Tactical Airlift Group, St. Joseph, Missouri
143rd  Tactical Airlift Group, Quonset Point, Rhode Island
145th  Tactical Airlift Group, Charlotte, North Carolina
153rd  Tactical Airlift Group, Cheyenne, Wyoming
164th  Tactical Airlift Group, Memphis, Tennessee
165th  Tactical Airlift Group, Savannah, Georgia
166th  Tactical Airlift Group, Wilmington, Delaware
167th  Tactical Airlift Group, Martinsburg, West Virginia
176th  Tactical Airlift Group, Anchorage, Alaska
179th  Tactical Airlift Group, Mansfield, Ohio
189th  Tactical Airlift Group, Little Rock, Arkansas
106th  Air Rescue and Recovery Group, Suffolk, New York
129th  Air Rescue and Recovery Group, Moffett NAS, California
105th  Military Airlift Group, Newburgh, New York
172nd  Military Airlift Group, Jackson, Mississippi
193rd  Special Operations Group, Middletown, Pennsylvania

## Pacific Air Forces

154th  Composite Group, Hickam AFB, Hawaii

## Strategic Air Command

101st  Air Refueling Wing, Bangor, Maine
126th  Air Refueling Wing, Chicago, Illinois
141th  Air Refueling Wing, Fairchild AFB, Washington
171th  Air Refueling Wing, Pittsburgn, Pennsylvania
128th  Air Refueling Group, Milwaukee, Wisconsin
134th  Air Refueling Group, Knoxville, Tennessee
151st  Air Refueling Group, Salt Lake City, Utah

157th  Air Refueling Group, Pease AFB, New Hampshire
160th  Air Refueling Group, Rickenbacker ANGB, Ohio
161st  Air Refueling Group, Phoenix, Arizona
170th  Air Refueling Group, McGuire AFB, New Jersey
189th  Air Refueling Group, Little Rock AFB, Arkansas
190th  Air Refueling Group, Forbes Field, Kansas

## Tactical Air Command

121st  Tactical Fighter Wing, Rickenbacker ANGB, Ohio
127th  Tactical Fighter Wing, Selfridge ANGB, Michigan
132nd  Tactical Fighter Wing, Des Moines, Iowa
140th  Tactical Fighter Wing, Buckley ANGB, Colorado
112th  Tactical Fighter Group, Pittsburgh, Pennsylvania
114th  Tactical Fighter Group, Sioux Falls, South Dakota
138th  Tactical Fighter Group, Tulsa, Oklahoma
150th  Tactical Fighter Group, Kirtland AFB, New Mexico
156th  Tactical Fighter Group, San Juan, Puerto Rico
162nd  Tactical Fighter Group, Tucson, Arizona
178th  Tactical Fighter Group, Springfield, Ohio
180th  Tactical Fighter Group, Toledo, Ohio
185th  Tactical Fighter Group, Sioux City, Iowa
192nd  Tactical Fighter Group, Byrd, Virginia
169th  Tactical Fighter Group, McEntire ANGB, South Carolina
128th  Tactical Fighter Wing, Truax, Wisconsin
174th  Tactical Fighter Wing, Syracuse, New York
103rd  Tactical Fighter Group, Bradley, Connecticut
104th  Tactical Fighter Group, Barnes, Massachusetts
175th  Tactical Fighter Group, Baltimore, Maryland
122nd  Tactical Fighter Wing, Ft. Wayne, Indiana
131st  Tactical Fighter Wing, St. Louis, Missouri
149th  Tactical Fighter Group, Kelly AFB, Texas
159th  Tactical Fighter Group, New Orleans NAS, Louisiana
163rd  Tactical Fighter Group, March AFB, California
181st  Tactical Fighter Group, Terre Haute, Indiana
188th  Tactical Fighter Group, Ft. Smith, Arkansas
108th  Tactical Fighter Wing, McGuire AFB, New Jersey
113th  Tactical Fighter Wing, Andrews AFB, Maryland
116th  Tactical Fighter Wing, Dobbins AFB, Georgia
158th  Tactical Fighter Group, Burlington, Vermont
183rd  Tactical Fighter Group, Springfield, Illinois
184th  Tactical Fighter Group, McConnell AFB, Kansas
187th  Tactical Fighter Group, Montgomery, Alabama
117th  Tactical Reconnaissance Wing, Birmingham, Alabama
123rd  Tactical Reconnaissance Wing, Louisville, Kentucky

124th  Tactical Reconnaissance Group, Boise, Idaho
152nd  Tactical Reconnaissance Group, Reno, Nevada
155th  Tactical Reconnaissance Group, Lincoln, Nebraska
186th  Tactical Reconnaissance Group, Meridian, Mississippi
110th  Tactical Air Support Group, Battle Creek, Michigan
111th  Tactical Air Support Group, Willow Grove NAS, Pennsylvania
182th  Tactical Air Support Group, Peoria, Illinois

# Index

## DATE DUE

| | | | |
|---|---|---|---|
| | | | |
| | | | |
| | | | |
| | | | |
| | | | |
| | | | |
| | | | |
| | | | |
| | | | |
| | | | |
| | | | |
| | | | |
| | | | |

MEDIALOG INC
ALEXANDRIA KY 41001